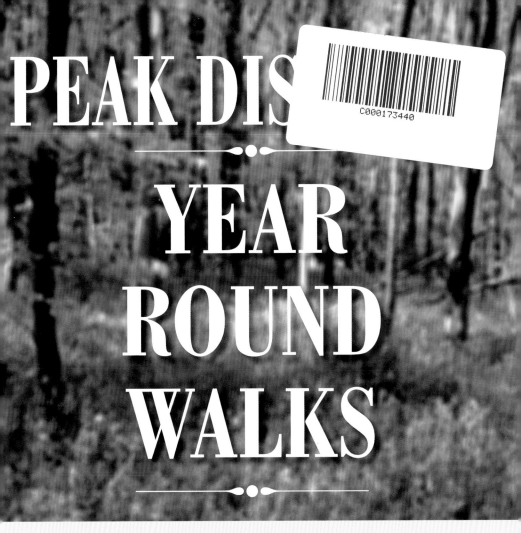

PEAK DIS
YEAR
ROUND
WALKS

Spring, Summer, Autumn & Winter

Peter Naldrett

COUNTRYSIDE BOOKS
NEWBURY BERKSHIRE

First published 2018
Text © 2018 Peter Naldrett

COUNTRYSIDE BOOKS
3 Catherine Road
Newbury
Berkshire

To view our complete range of books please visit us at
www.countrysidebooks.co.uk

ISBN 978 1 84674 355 9

Produced by The Letterworks Ltd., Reading
Typeset by KT Designs, St Helens
Printed by The Holywell Press, Oxford

Contents

Contents

Autumn

Winter

Introduction

Whenever you manage to pay a visit to the nation's oldest national park, you'll be rewarded with stunning scenery and some cracking facilities in its quaint villages. Whether it's a day trip, a holiday that lasts a week or more, or you live nearby, it's worth taking the time. And no matter where you're staying, there'll be a friendly welcome from locals and fellow travellers. It doesn't matter how long you come for, where you stay or how far you've travelled – there just isn't a bad time to visit the Peak District.

Each season offers something new in the Peaks. Winter brings a covering of snow on the hilltops, icy tree branches, clear blue skies and crisp, chilly mornings. With spring we see the emergence of new buds and the chance to pack our walking thermals away for another year. By the time summer comes, we're heading out in T-shirts and enjoying the purple carpet of heather blooming on the moors. And when the leaves fall in autumn, some terrific lowland walks share company with trees in a beautiful spectrum of colour. A stroll in the Peak District can be atmospheric at any time of year and in this book I have tried to capture specific places that shine at certain times in the calendar.

My love for the Peak District began in my teenage years and I have been a weekly visitor to this great location ever since. I now live on the edge of the national park and continue to count myself lucky that I can walk to a place with superb, inspiring views. It's a resource we must treasure and conserve so we do not ruin it for future generations. And it's a resource we should respect, so make sure you're taking Ordnance Survey maps and suitable clothing on these walks, along with sensible footwear, drinks, snacks and a GPS.

As you set out on these walks, I hope they bring you as much pleasure as they did for me and my friends and family joining me. We had many a fun, interesting and exciting day out preparing this book. From the awesome Derwent Valley to Carsington, from Hayfield to Eyam, there are 20 destinations in this book for you to explore, enjoying splendid views and learning about the local history along the way. The Peak District holds varied environments that shine at all times of year, and I wish you very happy ramblings as you make your way through woods, by reservoirs, up hills and down tracks.

Peter Naldrett
Twitter: @peternaldrett

For Nicola, Toby and Willow.

Acknowledgements
I would like to thank Nicola, Toby, Willow, Bingham, Jo, Mandy, Eve, Alison, Charlie and Paige for joining me on the walks.

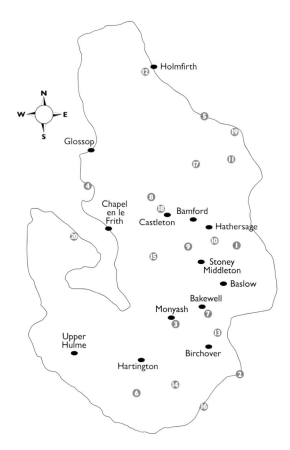

PUBLISHER'S NOTE

We hope that you obtain considerable enjoyment from this book; great care has been taken in its preparation. Although at the time of publication all routes followed public rights of way or permitted paths, diversion orders can be made and permissions withdrawn.

We cannot, of course, be held responsible for such diversion orders or any inaccuracies in the text which result from these or any other changes to the routes, nor any damage which might result from walkers trespassing on private property. We are anxious, though, that all the details covering the walks are kept up to date, and would therefore welcome information from readers which would be relevant to future editions.

The simple sketch maps that accompany the walks in this book are based on notes made by the author whilst surveying the routes on the ground. They are designed to show you how to reach the start and to point out the main features of the overall circuit, and they contain a progression of numbers that relate to the paragraphs of the text.

However, for the benefit of a proper map, we do recommend that you purchase the relevant Ordnance Survey sheet covering your walk. Ordnance Survey maps are widely available, especially through booksellers and local newsagents.

View from Owler Tor.

1 Longshaw Estate
2.1 miles/3.4km

Regular visitors to the Peak District will be familiar with the strange, isolated rocks that crown the peaty landscape. Standing like natural towers from the High Peak moors, these ancient gritstone tors are still dominant landmarks – long after the softer rock and material around them has been eroded. Pick a sunny day for this spring amble around the National Trust's Longshaw Estate and you'll be able to feed the ducks and enjoy a picnic close to some of these spectacularly-shaped rocks.

Time 1 hour.

Terrain Well-used paths, with some gentle inclines.

Starting point The National Trust car park at Longshaw. (Grid reference SK 266800).

How to get there & parking The A6187 runs between Hathersage and Sheffield. The National Trust's Longshaw Estate is located just to the east of Hathersage with the car park just off the A6187 near the Fox House pub. (**Sat nav** S11 7TZ).

Map Ordnance Survey OL1: The Peak District Dark Peak Area; Ordnance Survey OL24: The Peak District White Peak Area.

Refreshments The walk passes by the lovely National Trust café at Longshaw (☎ 01433 637904), and if it's a sunny day you'll probably see an ice cream van down at Padley Gorge.

The Walk _____

❶ From the car park, head down the path to the visitor centre, where you'll find a nice shop and café. From there, follow the sign for **Estate Walks** and head down towards the path, turning left onto it. When you pass through the gate, turn right onto the track with rhododendrons on either side. If you have young folk with you on the walk, there are some delightful little hideouts and play areas along this part of the route, all with a boggart theme. Indeed, **Boggart View** is soon found on the right.

❷ Go through another gate, and by now you'll be able to see the pond away on the right. The path bends round to the right and eventually meets the pond, where you may find a few ducks after crumbs from your picnic. Continue along this path, heading slightly downhill, and you'll be brought out at a road. Cross over and pick up the path directly across, heading for the bridge over **Burbage Brook**.

❸ Once over the bridge, head up the path straight ahead towards the large rocks in the distance. This is an optional detour on the route, but one which you really should take. Getting up close to one of the tors is a great experience and they also make an ideal spot for a picnic, whether providing a place to sit in the sun or sheltering you from wind. Return to the bridge when you've

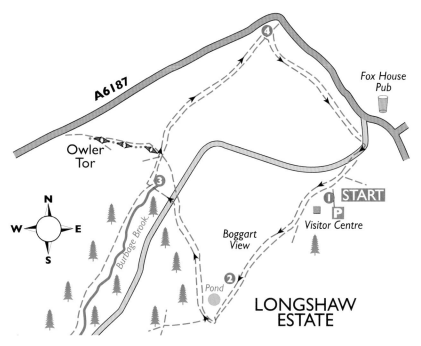

finished exploring the tor, and turn left to walk by the side of Burbage Brook. This is a lovely path which is very popular in good weather, with the brook picking up pace in some places as it descends from the Upper Burbage Valley, which you can see in the distance.

Mallard at Longshaw Estate lake.

4 When you meet a second footbridge over the river, cross it and take the path heading to the left up through the wood. The path crosses a stream and then bends back on itself to cross it again. Stick to this path and it will lead you out of the wood and to a gate at the main road. Cross over and pick up the track on the other side, which will bring you back to the visitor centre. A signed path on the left leads you back to the car park.

spring

What to look out for –

Owler Tor

Ask anyone about tors and they're likely to point you towards Dartmoor, a national park that has done a great job marketing these isolated wonders. But the Peak District is also one of the few places in the world where these landforms have taken shape, and this walk takes you to have a good look at Owler Tor. As you approach it, you'll be able to see the beautiful shape of the rocks that have been crafted by natural forces of weathering over thousands of years. Wind and rain play a part, but the sandy material that has been worn away from nearby rocks has also had a hand in it because the wind picks it up and hurls it against the tors to create a sandblasting effect. The unusually shaped landforms that result have led to locals giving some very inventive names to the tors in these parts – including Salt Cellar and Cakes of Bread!

Owler Tor.

Cromford Mill.

2 *Cromford*

3.7 miles/6km

Plan this glorious woodland walk for mid-April so you can catch the ocean of bluebells in full bloom as they bring the woods around Cromford to life. Derwent Valley Mills, where this walk starts, is on the list of World Heritage Sites, and the more you examine the history of the place, the more you realise it is thoroughly deserved. Cromford Mill was the first mill built in 1771 and can clearly be seen from the car park. See 'What to look out for' on page 14 for more details.

11

PEAK DISTRICT *Year Round Walks*

Time 1 hour 45 minutes.

Terrain Some steep ascents and descents through woodland and over fields.

Starting point Derwent Valley Mills car park, Cromford. (Grid reference SK 299571).

How to get there & parking Follow the A6 to Cromford and then turn off towards the train station. Derwent Valley Mills pay and display car park is on your left. (**Sat nav** DE4 3RQ).

Map Ordnance Survey OL24: The Peak District White Peak Area.

Refreshments Across the road from the car park on the first stretch of the walk, Wheatcroft's Wharf Café serves a range of food and drink. ☎ 01629 823265 www.cromfordmills.org.uk/wheatcrofts-wharf-dining.

The Walk _____

❶ From the car park, head for the road and turn left onto it, sticking to it as it bends left and crosses the **River Derwent**. The road then follows the course of the river and you'll be able to see it over the wall to your right. You'll pass **Cromford Station** and head under the railway bridge. Just after the bridge, take the path off to the left that enters a wood and get ready to start the climb up what is a fairly steep hill from the outset.

❷ After climbing up the hill, take the path off to the right through a gap in the stone wall. This is bluebell country and if you're here at the right time of year you'll be greeted by a carpet of blooming flowers on either side of the path. Leave the wood and enter a field, keeping to the main path that passes below **Meadow Wood Farm**. At the far side of the grassy field, your path will come out onto a small lane, where you should turn left and go up the hill. On reaching **Sunnybank**, take the path on the right that leads you into **Bow Wood**, another excellent place to admire and photograph bluebells. It's a Woodland Trust area and when you come to a fence and are faced with two paths you need to choose the one on the right.

❸ The woodland path leads you down the hill to a road; turn immediately left onto the small track and walk past the historic mill and factory buildings on your right. At the brow of the hill, take the path on the left signed for the

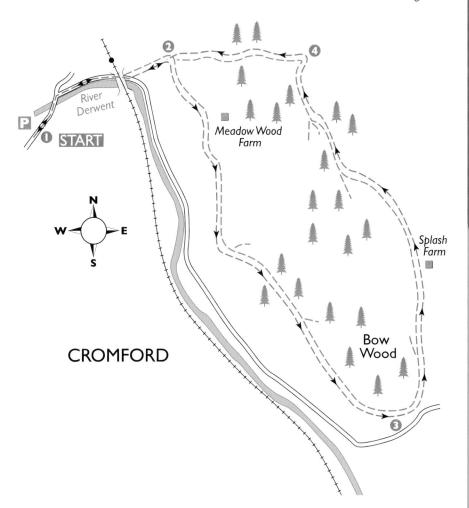

campsite and continue along here until you reach **Splash Farm**. Follow the track into the farm and look out for the path on the left that takes you beyond the buildings and into a field. You'll come to two paths and need to take the one on the left, clearing a stile and following the path into the field beyond. Stick to the right-hand side of the field. At the other side, head over a stile and you're back into the wood. Climb up the steep woodland path, turning right onto the next path when you meet it. Continue up and head through a gate, again turning right onto the bigger path you come across.

4 Shortly after, take the footpath off to the left that is marked by a signpost. From here, there is a steep descent through a wood and then over fields. Cross

spring

a stile, head across a track and continue down. Enter the wood for the last part of the descent and you'll be brought out onto the road you initially set out on. Turn right and follow the road back to the mills.

The woods at the start of the walk are home to a carpet of bluebells in spring.

What to look out for –

Cromford Mill

It may not be the most famous UNESCO World Heritage Site in the world, but the Derwent Valley Mills is hailed as one that changed the world because it saw the invention of the factory system and therefore pioneered the technique of manufacturing industry we take for granted today. It was the work of early industrialists Richard Arkwright, Jedediah Strutt and the Lombe Brothers that helped to make this site grow and become so inspirational to other parts of the world. With water-power being used on a large scale, silk throwing and cotton spinning thrived on this site. But because much of the textile industry was transferred to Lancashire and didn't continue in Derbyshire, the mills were not updated and redeveloped to the extent that others were. This means they can be explored today as exactly the same buildings that were constructed in the late 18th century. It costs £5 for an adult to gain access to the mills, with children going free, and it's well worth having a look at this well-preserved site that began humbly in the Derbyshire countryside and spread its influence out across continents. www.cromfordmills.org.uk

The white, winding limestone walls are a common feature in this part of the Peak District.

3 Monyash
3.6 miles/5.8km

The land you're standing on in Lathkill Dale used to be beneath a tropical sea. It's amazing to think about it as you stride around the grassy fields of Derbyshire, but fish were once swimming about where the grass now grows. Rarely does the natural history of an area come to life so vividly as here, where you're reminded at every turn of what life was like before the dinosaurs ruled the Earth. Enjoy the sight of spring flowers and new born lambs on this lovely round walk from a Derbyshire village in the heart of limestone country.

15

Time 2 hours.

Terrain Well-established paths, but take care over the limestone rocks which lie along the route in Lathkill Dale.

Starting point The eastern side of Monyash, at the northern entrance to Lathkill Dale. (Grid reference SK 157 665).

How to get there & parking Monyash is found on the B5055, with the A515 to the west and the A6 at Bakewell to the east. There is roadside parking on the eastern side of Monyash at the northern entrance to Lathkill Dale. There are toilets here too. (**Sat nav** DE45 1JG).

Map Ordnance Survey OL24: The Peak District White Peak Area.

Refreshments Walk into the centre of Monyash and you'll find The Old Smithy Tearoom, with a wide-ranging menu. ☎ 01629 810190. www.oldsmithymonyash.co.uk.

The Walk

❶ From your car, head along the road into **Monyash** until you reach the church, where you should take the footpath on your left.

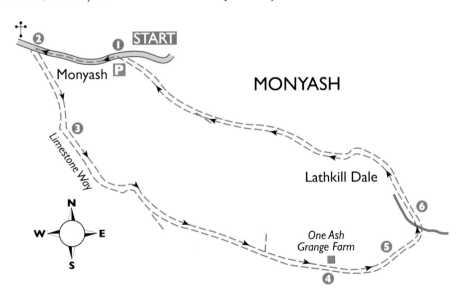

2 Continue to the far side of the churchyard and follow the path out beyond the wall, bringing you to a pleasant section of the walk across green fields.

3 After the path bends a little to the right, you come to a more substantial track that forms part of the **Limestone Way** long distance path. Turn left onto it at this point. This part of the Limestone Way is a wonderful place to walk, with limestone walls on either side and fabulous views beyond. When the track ends, go through the gate and make your way across **Fern Dale**. When you come to the National Trust sign, take the path off to the right signed for the Limestone Way. Press on through fields and pass through another gate, again following the Limestone Way on a well-established route. As this long-distance path progresses, the route switches to the other side of the limestone wall and heads through more gates.

4 On reaching **One Ash Grange Farm**, turn left onto the **Limestone Way** and follow the sign for **Lathkill Dale**. At the other side of the farm, the path takes you down some steps and you begin the descent that will take you into this fantastic valley. Pass through a gate and then the descent gets steeper and

spring

rockier, down and down towards **Lathkill Dale** and you pass some dramatic limestone cliffs along the way.

5 There is a junction of paths at the bottom of the hill; take the one on the left towards **Lathkill Dale**. There's some rocky ground to pass through and the vegetation starts to differ as you get into **Lathkill Dale**. When you reach the footbridge, head straight across and turn left.

6 After leaving the footbridge, the rest of the walk is a wonderful stroll through **Lathkill Dale** itself. It's a very distinct dale, hemmed in by steep sides. There are wonderful limestone scree slopes off to the right, with cliffs at the top where the smaller pieces of rock have fallen off over centuries of freeze-thaw weathering. The journey continues up **Lathkill Dale**, beyond spring flowers and limestone outcrops. When you pass through a gate there is a change in the landscape, with the rocks giving way to a scene of greener fields. Another gate leads you onto a track which takes you all the way up to the road where the walk set out from.

What to look out for –

The limestone in Lathkill Dale

Due to the movement of the Earth's plates, caused by convection currents beneath the surface, the continents on our planet slowly move around. What we now know as Derbyshire used to be a lot further south and stood beneath warm tides where fish and crustaceans  made their home. When those ocean-going animals died, their bodies drifted to the seabed and were crushed and compacted over time to form the rock we call limestone. And so the limestone you see on this walk is jam-packed full of fossils that reflect the teeming sea life of yesteryear – some 350 million years ago, experts reckon. In the limestone scree slopes of Lathkill Dale there are bound to be some recently broken rocks and it's worth examining them to look for fossils; finding one on your own is a real delight. If you don't manage to see any fossils in the limestone when you're out and about, check out the rock you pass over at the start of the walk when you enter the church grounds because it's full of them. And if you walk into Monyash be sure to have a nosy at the entrance to the pub; the stone flooring as you go through the door is mesmerising.

Bluebell Wood

4 Hayfield
4.7 miles/7.6km

You'll step out on the Sett Valley Trail and the Pennine Bridleway on this peaceful round walk that takes you to a delightful carpet of spring bluebells and the picturesque village of Hayfield. Bluebell Wood is the main reason people come here, in order to experience the festival of bluebells that lasts a few weeks in the spring. However, there is also plenty to see during the rest of the year. Stoats, mice and weasels live in the wood, with badgers and deer also passing through. Wild flowers include wood anemone and marsh marigolds, while the many tree species include oak, maple and willow. It's a superb place and a real highlight of the walk.

PEAK DISTRICT *Year Round Walks*

Time 2 hours.

Terrain Well-established paths with some steep inclines.

Starting point Sett Valley Trail car park. (Grid reference SK 036869).

How to get there & parking Hayfield is on the western edge of the Peak District, situated on the main A624 road. Sett Valley Trail is well signed from the A624 at Hayfield and there is a large pay and display car park from which to base your day out. (**Sat nav** SK22 2ES).

Map Ordnance Survey OL1: The Peak District Dark Peak Area.

Refreshments At the end of the route, you'll walk along Church Street and discover Millie's Tea Rooms. ☎ 01663 741584. Postcode SK22 2JE. www.millieshayfield.co.uk.

The Walk

1 Head over to the start of the **Sett Valley Trail**, pass through the gate and set off along the trail. Before long you'll come to an entrance into **Bluebell Wood** on your right. It's well worth heading into this looping walk extension for a look around in April or May when the bluebells are out. The carpet of flowers within this nature reserve is superb and it's a great place to take some photographs. Continue along the trail in the wood, following the duckboards, and you'll be brought back to the **Sett Valley Trail**.

2 When you've finished exploring in the wood, turn right on the trail and carry on. The whole valley soon opens up in front of you and you can enjoy the view of **Lantern Pike** on your right, with the **River Sett** running down in the valley below. You'll pass a picnic area on the right, which gives you an awesome spot to enjoy a rest or a bite to eat. And then, shortly after, you'll see **Birch Vale Reservoir** down to your right, with its unusual island in the middle of the water. Sticking to the **Sett Valley Trail**, continue ahead and leave the view over the reservoir behind you.

3 Before long you come to a road at what used to be **Birch Vale Station**. There's a sharp right-hand turn and you should follow the bumpy path down the hill. When you're brought out onto the road at the bottom of the hill, continue heading down the road and cross over the **River Sett**.

4 Take the bridleway on the right at the other side of the river. This is the **Pennine Bridleway**, a long-distance route, and you should stay on it as it heads up the hill and brings you out at a small, country road. Cross over and pick up the bridleway at the other side, following the well-defined track and **Pennine Bridleway** signs as it climbs the hill and skirts around the edge of Lantern Pike. Beyond the brow of the hill, the bridleway starts a descent across fields and brings you to a junction at **Blackshaw Farm** where six paths meet.

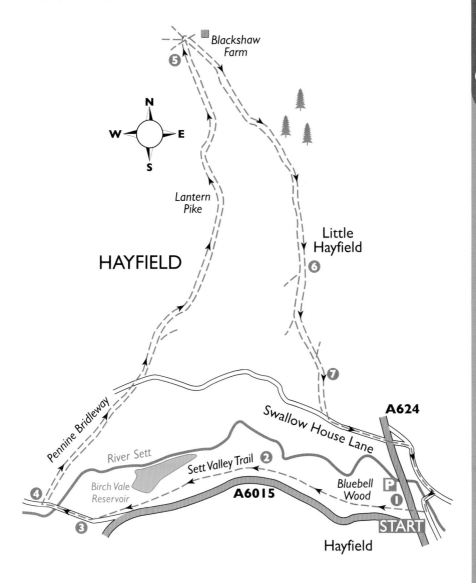

spring

spring

Look out for the island in the middle of the reservoir, visible from the Sett Valley Trail.

5 Of all the options, you need the path that almost doubles back on itself and turns to the right, leading you away from the farm. This continues to go downhill and joins up with another path before proceeding by the village of **Little Hayfield**, which you can see to the left.

6 Stick to the main path as you head away from **Little Hayfield**, with a small wood on your left. As the path forks in two, take the route to your left towards **Hayfield**.

7 Follow this path and it will soon turn into **Bank Vale Road**, with the start of Hayfield's housing appearing on either side. At the main road, turn left onto **Swallow House Lane** and continue ahead, under the A624. At the T-junction, turn right onto **Market Street** and continue ahead into the lovely village of **Hayfield**. When **Market Street** bends to the right it turns into **Church Street** and soon after crossing the **River Sett** you should take **Walk Mill Road** on the right. From here you will see the crossing that will take you to the other side of the A624 and back to the **Sett Valley Trail car park**.

What to look out for –

Bluebell Wood Local Nature Reserve

If you time it right when you go down to the woods, you're sure of a big surprise. Tackle this walk in April and May and there'll be thousands of

bluebells flowering, so take your camera and allow plenty of time to stop and enjoy. The spring wonder takes place in the aptly named Bluebell Wood, a nature reserve you'll come across after only a few metres of this walk but one which will provide lasting memories. When you see the turning on the right for the 1,100-metre circular route, your magical experience will begin almost immediately. Accessibility is the key in Bluebell Wood; the path for the public has been upgraded in such a fashion that it's possible for pushchairs and wheelchairs to get all the way around. Duckboards to negotiate the trickiest surfaces have been made out of recycled plastic to ensure they last as long as possible and aren't sitting in a landfill for years to come.

The path around the edge of Langsett Reservoir is flanked by pine trees which have a rich aroma.

5 Langsett
4 miles/6.4km

This lovely spring walk takes you through gorgeous pine woodland, around a delightful reservoir and out onto remote moorland. Langsett Reservoir was constructed between 1898 and 1904 and is surrounded by oak and birch trees which have been planted to create woodland and provide habitat for indigenous wildlife. In 2007, a pond was built near Brookhouse Bridge, at the reservoir's western end, to encourage colonies of frogs and newts. You'll also get to see bluebells and ferns emerging as the season comes to life.

The Facts

Time 2 hours 30 minutes.

Terrain Well-established paths, with some rough ground and steep inclines.

Starting point Langsett Reservoir car park. (Grid reference SE 210005).

How to get there & parking Langsett is found on the A616, on the eastern edge of the Peak District, north-west of Stocksbridge. There is a decent sized free car park at Langsett Reservoir, along with public toilets. An overflow car park is available further along the main road. (**Sat nav** S36 4GY).

Map Ordnance Survey OL1: The Peak District Dark Peak Area.

Refreshments The distinctively spotty Bank View Café is on the main road near the car park. ☎ 01226 762337 www.bankviewcafe.co.uk. Postcode S36 4GY.

The Walk

1 With your back to the A616 in the car park, head to the far-right corner and pick up the path that takes you down the slope towards the water's edge. Turn right when you reach the path at the side of **Langsett Reservoir**, and carry on ahead as you move away from the dam wall. When you reach the path near the water, turn right onto it and at spring time you'll find yourself in a blooming paradise of bluebells and emerging ferns. This is a fabulous pine tree woodland, which eventually turns into an area of silver birches.

2 As you reach the end of the reservoir, leave the waterside to enter the woods. There is a substantial cobbled track you need to take that heads left and proceeds down to the river. Cross the bridge and turn left at the other side, though you may want to take advantage of this glorious location to have a spring picnic. The path you follow now is signed for **Derwent and Ashop Valley** and you've got Langsett Woods immediately next to the path; you're actually near an area known as North America for the similarities it has with the forested areas across the Atlantic. The path starts to climb and meander its way up the hill, heading out onto the moor and leaving the trees behind. As you walk up to higher ground you'll notice the heather, and as you glance down to the left there's a great view of **Langsett Reservoir**.

spring

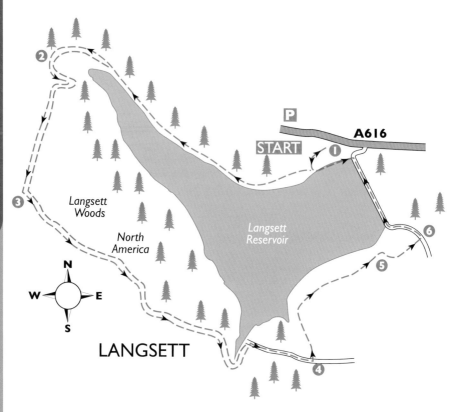

❸ When you reach a junction of paths, turn left onto the bridleway. This takes you past two old, ruined buildings and through a gate. The path then heads back down the hill towards the woods; it is uneven in parts so care is needed. Go through another gate and continue along this main path.

❹ Just before the path leads you to a road, look for the small path on the left marked by a blue sign. Follow this permissive route, which branches off to the left until you wind up once more at the path beside the reservoir.

❺ After sticking to the reservoir for a while, the path veers off into the woods and climbs the hill; stick to the fence initially and follow this path up. You'll eventually leave the fence and follow the path deeper into the woods, away from the reservoir. It will bring you out at the far corner, where you join the road at the point it meets a track.

The path with Langsett Reservoir on your left.

spring

6 Head to the road and turn left onto it, following it down the hill and across the dam wall. At the far side of the dam wall, take the path off to the left and begin walking on the path with the reservoir on the left. Look for the track leading up the hill to the right, which will take you back to the car park.

What to look out for –

Memories of the Tour de France

When the opening stages of the Tour de France were held in Yorkshire during the summer of 2014, few would have thought the legacy would be so long-lasting and profound. They were a very special couple of days in these parts of Yorkshire, with thousands of people lining the streets before the best long-distance cyclists in the world hurtled by at breakneck speed. Langsett featured on Day 2 – the final day in Yorkshire before the event moved to London, and then France. The cyclists hurried down the A616, turning off near here at Midhope before going over the hills to Bradfield and finishing off in Sheffield city

centre. Years later, the villages in these parts are still immensely proud of their involvement on that fabulous, busy day, when festivals were held every few miles along the route and a significant number of families gained a lust for cycling that still endures. As you drive along the route it's possible to see some of the words of encouragement painted onto the road, and the trademark yellow bikes are still visible. At Langsett, look out for the sign at the bar of the pub featuring a crest made up of different Tour de France jerseys. The most prominent feature for miles around, though, is Bank View Café on the main road close to the starting point. To celebrate the biking event, the café was painted white and covered with red spots to match the "King of the Mountains" jersey given to the rider who tackles the climbs triumphantly. It's a very popular spot for cyclists to stop off at and have a break, including those not so great at getting up the demanding Peak District inclines.

On the first half of the walk you'll enjoy views of rolling countryside before descending into Dovedale.

6 Dovedale

4.8 miles/7.7km

No visit to Dovedale would be complete without a hop over the famous stepping stones that have made this place picture-postcard perfect since the 19th century. Enjoy a picnic by the stepping stones on the River Dove, taking in one of the most quintessentially English scenes in the Peak District.

Time 2 hours 30 minutes.

Terrain Some steep climbs and a descent you'll need to take care on.

Starting point The centre of Ilam. (Grid reference SK 135508).

How to get there & parking Ilam is a small village to the north of Ashbourne, between the A523 and the A515. Parking is available in the centre of the village and there is also a large National Trust car park at Ilam Hall. (**Sat nav** DE6 2AZ).

Map Ordnance Survey OL24: The Peak District White Peak Area.

Refreshments The Manifold Tea Room at the National Trust's Ilam Hall is a short walk from the centre of Ilam and a good place for refreshments. ☎ 01335 350503. www.nationaltrust.org.uk/ilam-park-dovedale-and-the-white-peak .

The Walk _____

❶ From your car, make your way to the centre of the village and find the memorial that stands tall on the main road. Follow the road that leads off opposite the memorial, signed for the **Isaak Walton Hotel**. Take the footpath on the left that leads onto access land and take the route on the left that takes you directly up the hill. Head over the stile and continue up the incline, with **Bunster Hill** rising on your right. This is a steep climb, rewarded by the fantastic views you earn the further up you go. Head over another stile and press on up, with the path, sticking close to the limestone wall on your left.

❷ The land levels when you reach a National Trust sign announcing Bunster Hill on the right – at this point you need to go in the opposite direction, taking the path to the left. This is a well-used path and again there is a wall on your left. The path develops into a more substantial track and heads towards **Ilam Tops Farm**.

❸ On reaching the farm, take the path on the right that heads down towards **Dovedale**. You'll soon be walking towards a house and need to take the path on the right that is signed for Dovedale once more. There's an unmissable solitary gate in the middle of the field and the path goes beyond this, soon bending round to the left. When you reach the signpost, take the path on the left and look out for the limestone outcrops you can see on the left. Continue along

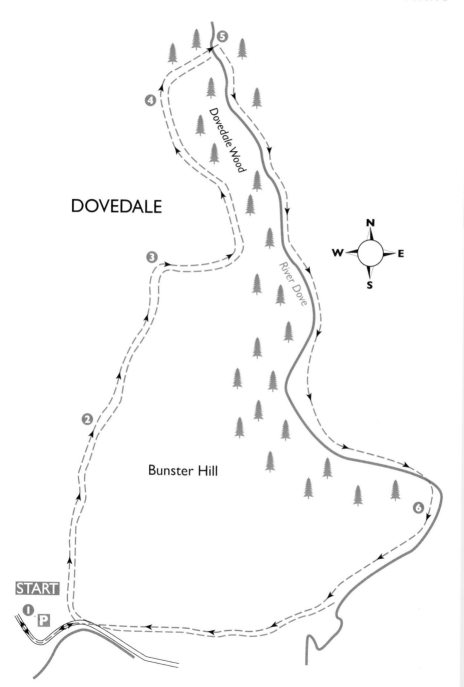

DOVEDALE

Doveddale Wood

River Dove

Bunster Hill

START

N
W E
S

On long, warm summer days there's often time for a paddle in the River Dove.

this path, taking care as there's a big drop down on the right. Keep an eye out beyond the trees on the right as you get the occasional glimpse of Dovedale and the magnificent limestone features that are to be seen later.

④ After crossing a field, you come to a wall and need to head through the gate taking you into **Dovedale Wood**. The path then begins a descent which is quite steep in places. Take care on this section of the walk as the path can be slippery and there are rocks to contend with as well. The path down is obvious and keeps heading left at first – ignore the rough track heading down in a more direct route. You'll soon reach a series of wooden steps on a steep section, with the path continuing to wind its way down afterwards. Take care as both the steps and the rocks can be slippery.

⑤ At the bottom of the hill you will come to another set of wooden steps. Turn right at the bottom and make your way across the footbridge, paying full attention to the limestone pinnacle **Pickering Tor**. At the other side of the river, turn right onto the track and begin a section of the walk that sticks by the edge of the **River Dove**. Look out for the impressive cave on the left as well as the stream emerging from nearby, then walk over the wooden boards. The path leaves the river and heads up some steps on a little climb. This is a great place to look out for fossils on the rocks. Head back down the other side of the little hill and rejoin the path near the river.

6 Walk through the gap in the wall and cross over the picturesque stepping stones, turning left at the other side of the river. Follow this path by the river until you come to the car park; during this stretch you will have come across a couple of places to buy nice ice cream! At the car park, go towards the road and then take the path that leads into the field opposite. Stick to this as it rises over the hill and goes to the right of the hill. Cross over the fields and the path will drop down to the left, bringing you out at a road. Turn right onto it and you'll return to the centre of Ilam.

What to look out for –

The stepping stones at Dovedale

Like many instances where people have altered the countryside landscape, the stepping stones did not have an instant appeal but over the decades they have become strongly associated with this quaint, beautiful valley. In truth, you don't have to go over the stepping stones to get to the other side because there is a bridge a little further down the valley towards Ilam. But where's the fun in that? In the summer months, it's quite normal to see people queueing for some time until it's their turn to head across. People can only make the journey across the River Dove in single file and so there

can be a fair bit of congestion at either side, but it's something you just have to do! On rare occasions, storms leading to rising river levels and flooding have swept away the stones and led to significant damage. There have been times when the popular tourist cross-river route has had to be closed off. But it's always been worth investing money to get the stepping stones renovated and the picturesque scene back to its best. The fossil-laden stepping stones are one of the main reasons this remote dale has the high number of visitors that it does.

Chatsworth House.

7 *Bakewell and Chatsworth*

7.5 miles /12km

The historic parkland around Chatsworth House is discovered on this beautiful summer walk that is ideal for the long days in June and July. This is a challenging walk, and one that is incredibly rewarding on a long summer day. The two climbs over the hill between Bakewell and Chatsworth are the toughest moments, but each yields a lovely view and an easy downhill section.

The Facts

Time 4 hours.

Terrain A challenging walk with some tough climbs.

Starting point The former Bakewell train station, at the car park for the popular Monsal Trail. (Grid reference SK 222689).

How to get there & parking Once in Bakewell, turn off the A619 onto Station Road and you'll find the car park at the top. (**Sat nav** DE45 1GE).

Map Ordnance Survey OL24: The Peak District White Peak Area.

Refreshments When you walk through the village of Edensor, look out for the lovely Tea Cottage. ☎ 01246 582315. www.edensorteacottage.co.uk.

The Walk

1 Set off from what was once Bakewell Station, now the delightful setting of the **Monsal Trail**. There are likely to be cyclists as well as walkers here, so take care. Follow the signs for Coombs Road and press on along what is a largely flat route. The route takes you under a couple of bridges that once carried traffic over the railway line. From here, you can enjoy views over Bakewell down to your right. This is a nice, easy section and it takes you to one end of the Monsal Trail, so when you reach **Coombs Road**, make your way down the path to your right.

2 There's an impressive viaduct overhead that trains once travelled over, but you should take care and watch for cars as you make your way across the road and pick up the bridleway on the other side. There are trees on your left and there's a bit of a climb before it levels out. Look out for a bridleway you soon need to take on the right. Continue ahead down here, looking out for a bridleway on the left.

3 Take the bridleway and follow it as it leads to a bowling green. This section of the path can be challenging as it is fairly rocky and has a steady incline. You'll eventually get brought out at a country road, where you need to turn left and press on up the hill. As the road bends to the left, you can see the disused railway line on the right and the tunnel that it entered before going onto the Haddon Hall estate. This tunnel was not dug through a hill. It was built with

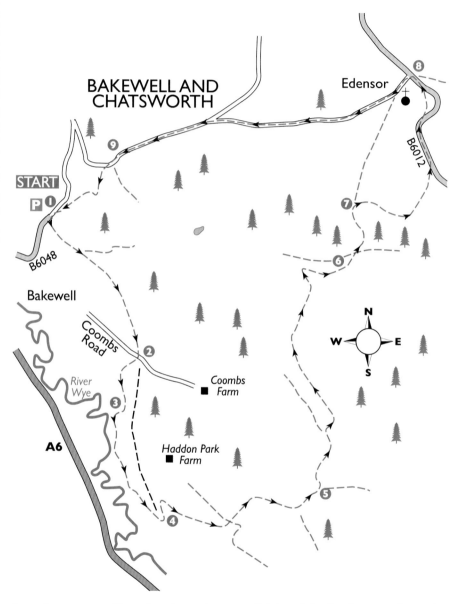

BAKEWELL AND
CHATSWORTH

Edensor

START

Bakewell

Coombs
Road

River
Wye

Coombs
Farm

Haddon Park
Farm

A6

the sole purpose of keeping the trains out of sight of the landowner, the Duke of Rutland.

④ Take the bridleway that turns off to the right. Head along a small path and pass through a gate. You'll eventually come out at a track; follow this up the hill, which is tough at first but soon levels out and then goes down into a dip. When you reach the T-junction of paths, turn left and go down the hill until you reach another junction where there are different bridleways to choose from. You now have to come off the track and head along the bridleway signed for **Chatsworth**.

Edensor.

5 This is a very steep section through the woods, bringing you out at a more substantial track and continuing to climb. It's a very strenuous and demanding climb, but it will eventually level out and come to a pleasant section and then through a gap in an old dry-stone wall. Continue through the trees and pass through a gate before entering a field where you follow the track down a steep section of the route. Follow the track across the field to the other side, where you'll go through another gate and turn immediately right, continuing to go downhill.

6 When you reach the intersection soon after, turn left and press on up the small hill and across the field. You'll soon reach a gate taking you into a wood; follow the track through here and when you come out at the other side you'll see Chatsworth House.

7 Continue down the hill and follow the markers until you get to the road that passes through the estate. Turn left here and stick to the track at the side of the road – this means you won't actually need to go on the road and you'll also actually nicely cut out the corner. The track brings you to **Edensor**, the small village you can see from some distance away thanks to the church.

8 Go through the gate into the village and follow the road around to the right – although you may want to stop off at the tea rooms on the left! As you follow the road around, you'll pass a row of houses and then the road turns into a track which begins a tough uphill climb. Continue ahead all the way up the

track. You'll come out at a road; continue to follow this up the hill.

9 Just beyond the brow of the hill, the road bends to the right and there is a track heading straight on towards **Bakewell**. Follow this path down the steep hill and across the golf course, where it will bring you out onto a road. Head down the hill and take the approach to the old station on the right to reach the point you set out from.

What to look out for –

Chatsworth House

The wonderful parkland at Chatsworth is a fantastic place to explore, whether it's gazing at ancient trees, meandering to Edensor village or gazing at the hunting tower. It is a truly inspiring landscape, worked on by Capability Brown and with many of his features surviving to this day. He straightened the river flowing past the house and added many of the trees that are still planted around the grounds to improve the quality of the view. He also moved the village of Edensor to its present location, so that the houses could not be seen from the windows of Chatsworth. But it is the actual house that commands the most respect and dominates the parkland as soon as it comes into view. In the early 20th century, alterations to tax collection and a wave of social change put a lot of pressure on grand country houses such as Chatsworth. Unlike many similar houses, Chatsworth has survived as the family home of the Duke and Duchess of Devonshire through 16 generations of the Cavendish family. Today, it generates money from allowing visitors into the house, garden and farmyard, where there is a great playground for children. The house is extremely popular at Christmas, when each year it is decorated with a different theme and opens its doors to coach parties and family daytrippers from all over the country. There are many splendid rooms to look at inside, but if you don't fancy entering the house make sure you give it a good examination from the outside. There are many important people who have been here and shared the view, including Queen Victoria. You can absorb the history of this country house as you wander through the park.

Mam Tor view.

8 Edale

4 miles/6.4km

Dark Peak meets White Peak atop Mam Tor, with far-reaching views of gritstone moors and limestone farms being the reward for climbing this Peak District favourite. To the south is Limestone Country, beginning at Castleton with its caverns and access to the Limestone Way. And to the north lies Kinder Scout, the tallest peak in the national park, where a peaty plateau sits high above the picturesque village of Edale.

Time 2 hours 15 minutes.

Terrain Some steep climbs up to Mam Tor.

Starting point The main car park at Edale. (Grid reference SK 124853).

How to get there & parking The road to Edale is signed off the A6187 from the village of Hope, which sits between Castleton and Hathersage. The car park is in the centre of the village. (**Sat nav** S33 7ZL).

Map Ordnance Survey OL1: The Peak District Dark Peak Area.

Refreshments The Penny Pot café at Edale is run by the National Trust and found close to the car park, on the way to the train station. ☎ 01433 670293 www.nationaltrust.org.uk/kinder-edale-and-the-dark-peak.

The Walk

1 From the car park, head to the main road you have just travelled along and turn left onto it. Take the path on the right signed for **Castleton and Hope**. Head down the slope as the path takes you down to the river. Cross over and follow the track up the other side. Pass some farm building and, as you climb, be sure to look behind to see **Kinder Scout**.

2 Before you arrive at a house, the path branches off to the right and there is a gate in the wall you need to go through. Press on up the grassy hillside, with a steep section taking you onwards to **Hollins Cross**.

3 At Hollins Cross you come to a very well-established and frequently used path running along the ridge from left to right. Turn right onto it and you'll see **Mam Tor**, which is your destination in the distance. It's a steady climb, but the path is good and there is grass at the side should you feel the need to rest. When you reach the top the trig point welcomes you for a photograph and some time to reflect on the magnificent views over **Kinder Scout** and the **Hope Valley**. From the summit, proceed straight ahead on the path as it descends on the other side.

4 When you reach the road, turn right onto it until you reach the path on the right that leads you back into the access land. There are two paths and you need the one on the left that heads straight down the hill at the side of the road. Enjoy the summer heather that you will see around here. Pass the steep

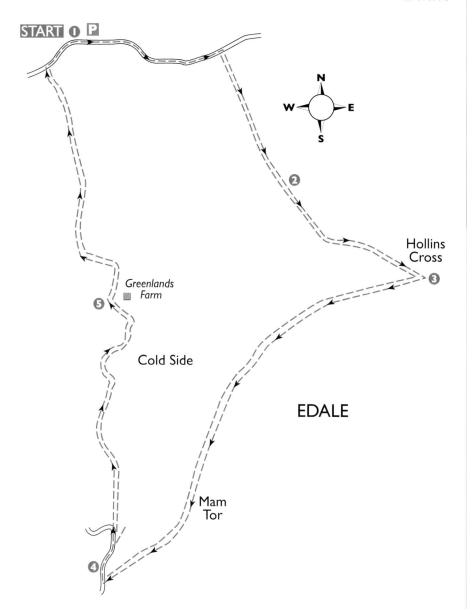

edge of **Cold Side** on your right and then you go through a gate into an area of wooded farmland.

5 At **Greenlands Farm**, turn right and follow the track that goes around it. When you get to another gate, head through it and you'll be on a concrete track

summer

you need to follow all the way down the hill to **Edale**. This will bring you out at the main road once again. Turn right and you'll soon be back at the car park where you started.

What to look out for –

Mam Tor

When you reach the triangulation pillar at the summit of Mam Tor, you're treated to a 360° view in a dramatic part of the Peak District. The pillar here, known as a trig point, was part of a network of over 6,000 similar concrete structures placed on the highest parts of the British landscape by the Ordnance Survey in the 1930s. By placing a theodolite into the top and triangulating with other trig points, surveyors were able to piece together the O.S. maps people use to plot their route. Today, people love to have a picture taken with the trig point because it shows they have reached the top of the hill. It's

Trig point on Mam Tor.

also a popular place for people to have a summit picnic. These concrete pillars are the historical equivalent of our GPS system.

Standing on top of Mam Tor at 517m above sea level, you won't be able to see the side of the mountain that slipped away during landslides in the 1970s. The sheer edge of Mam Tor is clearly visible from Castleton and the surrounding countryside, though, so stop to have a look if you pass through the village. The landslide was caused by unstable layers of shale and resulted in so much damage to the road below that it was closed for good. Today, the former route between Hathersage and Manchester can be visited and gives the impression that this is an area prone to earthquakes.

The small plantation of pines you pass on leaving Eyam Moor.

9 Eyam

4.4 miles/7km

The summer months are ideal for a wander onto the moors above Eyam before rewarding yourself with an ice cream and a visit to the village's craft shops. The village is also known for the incredible story of sacrifice during 1665-66 when the villagers suffered huge mortality rates due to the bubonic plague. The church of St Lawrence and Eyam museum are both very informative if you'd like to find out more about this beautiful village's dark past.

Time 2 hours 30 minutes.

Terrain Some steep paths and uneven ground.

Starting point Eyam Hall car park. (Grid reference SK 215764).

How to get there & parking To the north of Chatsworth, the village of Eyam is signed off the A623 close to Stoney Middleton. Follow the signs for Eyam Hall. The car park is pay and display. (**Sat nav** S32 5QW).

Map Ordnance Survey OL24: The Peak District White Peak Area.

Refreshments The Buttery Café is located in the craft centre at Eyam Hall, selling hot drinks, meals and cream teas. ☎ 01433 630505.

The Walk

1 From the car park, head for the road junction, and turn left to walk up **Church Street**. If you come here towards the end of summer – on or just after the August bank holiday – you'll be in time to see the village's well dressing. This is a tradition that sees water sources decorated with ornate pictures made of flowers and is worth the small detour if you see it signed off to the right.

2 When you continue up **Church Street**, take the path you see on the right and follow the signs that take you through a gate and across a field. You'll be brought out at a cottage; turn left here and then right, sticking to the footpath signs. A steep section of the route follows, climbing the hill, passing ferns and trees along the way. The path eventually bends to the right, crossing a stream and passing through a series of gates to bring you out at a track. Turn left onto it.

3 On reaching the road, turn right and head along it for around 250 metres. Take the path on the left and press on up the hill, passing through different fields and making your way up to **Sir William Hill Road**. Cross over when you get to it, and take the path opposite. You're now on **Eyam Moor** and the landscape has changed significantly, with the peaty ground supporting the lovely summer pinks of the Peak District heather. A couple of cairns mark the path to follow and soon after the route begins to head downhill. The path heads beyond the plantation of trees on the left, coming to a junction of four pathways at the bottom near the wall.

4 Take the route on the left, almost doubling back on yourself. This path takes you on the left side of the **Gotherage Plantation**. You are then led over a wall and the path cuts between the trees and continues up the other side of the plantation. Ignore the path on the right and continue straight ahead on the path, joining a more established track after passing the farm on your left. When you meet a larger track passing in front of you, turn left onto it.

5 The track soon brings you to a small country lane, where you need to

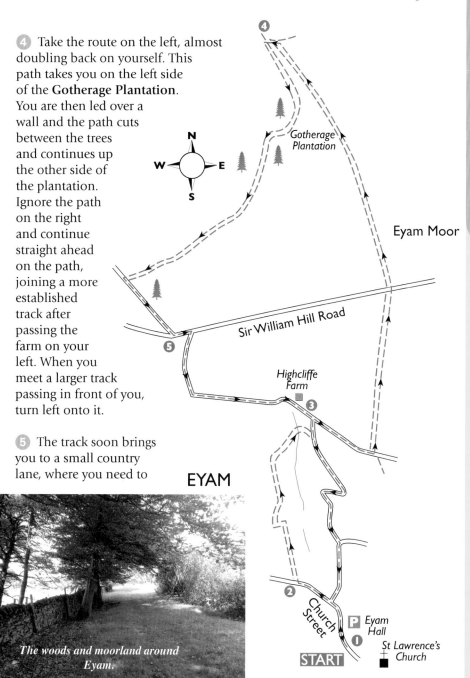

EYAM

The woods and moorland around Eyam.

Gotherage Plantation

Eyam Moor

Sir William Hill Road

Highcliffe Farm

Church Street

P   Eyam Hall

❶

START

✝ St Lawrence's Church

turn left once again. Follow the road around to the right and continue ahead, bending sharply to the left soon after. Continue down the road for half a kilometre until you reach **Highcliffe Barn**, where you need to turn right and begin to walk down the byway. This is a well-established track to follow, although there are some rocks along the way so take care on this stretch. It winds a gentle way down and comes out in the village. Turn right onto **Edge Road** and head into the centre of **Eyam**, turning left onto the village's main road to get back to **Eyam Hall**.

What to look out for –

St Lawrence's Church

The church of St Lawrence in the centre of Eyam houses a really informative display about the dark days when the plague ripped the village apart. It's a great place to learn about the unique story of selfless villagers in frightening times doing their best to stop its spread. While the plague raged in London during 1665, rural Derbyshire may have seemed like a good place to live. But when tailor George Viccars ordered cloth from the capital it arrived damp. When it was laid out to dry, plague-carrying fleas were released and Viccars was dead within days. Over the next 14 months, 260 lives were lost in the village. But the folk of Eyam ensured the plague did not spread elsewhere in Derbyshire by placing themselves in quarantine. Nobody was allowed into Eyam and none of the local residents took it upon themselves to leave. Food and medical supplies were left on the hills surrounding Eyam at the boundary of the village. The church, where people now learn about these historic events, was closed and no services took place there during the troubled times.

Instead, church gatherings were held in the nearby valley of Cucklett Delf, where a plague commemoration service is still held once a year.

The wooden footbridge over Burbage Brook is framed by a horizon of dramatic tors.

10 Grindleford

3.8 miles/6.1km

A delightful stroll through Padley Gorge along the banks of Burbage Brook, a popular haunt for families in the summer months. The walk leads you through ancient woodland and the wildlife-rich valley before entering the National Trust's Longshaw Estate with its spectacular Peak District views.

47

Time 2 hours.

Terrain Some rocky ground on this walk, which has a steep start and finish.

Starting point Station Approach, the road heading towards Grindleford Station. (Grid reference SK 251787).

How to get there & parking Grindleford is located between Hathersage and Calver in the Peak District. Head north from Grindleford along the B6521, following signs for the station. Park near the station, or alternatively arrive by train. (**Sat nav** S32 2JA).

Map Ordnance Survey OL1: The Peak District Dark Peak Area, Ordnance Survey OL24: The Peak District White Peak Area.

Refreshments Grindleford Station Café is at the walk's start and finish point, close to the train station. ☎ 01433 631011.

The Walk

① Make your way to the Grindleford Station Café. This is a great place to get a tea or coffee (served in either half pints or pints) and a hearty snack. From nearby you get a good view down to the train station. Look out also for the **Totley Tunnel**, which swallows trains as they leave here and head towards Sheffield. The path you need to take heads up the hill to the right of the café. It's a steep climb and brings you out at a road, where you should turn left.

② Look out for the footpath on the left, taking you into the National Trust land at **Padley Gorge**. Keep to the main path heading through the wood, ignoring the small path that leads off down the hill. The path is fairly wide and easy to keep a track of, all the time leading you by summer ferns that are on either side and a range of deciduous trees. Pass a solitary gatepost remaining in the middle of the path and, before long, the river comes into view down on the left. This is **Burbage Brook**, a tributary that runs down to the **River Derwent**. The path leads you back up, close to the road, and there are a couple of dips to negotiate as you head over small streams. Head back down towards the river, cross over a ruined dry-stone wall and follow the main path until you reach a wall with a wooden gate. Head through here, noting that the ground becomes rocky.

③ Cross the wooden footbridge and turn right, following the riverside route

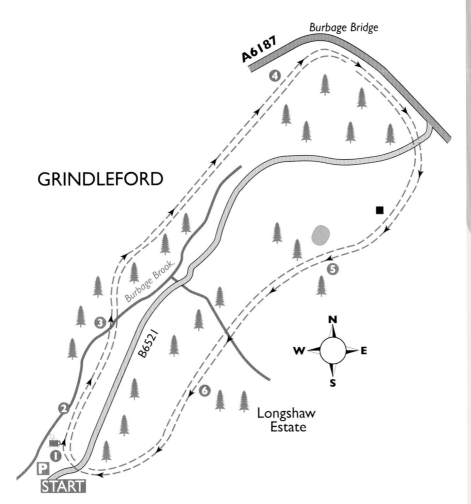

Burbage Bridge

A6187

GRINDLEFORD

Burbage Brook.

B6521

Longshaw
Estate

N
W E
S

START

summer

further up the valley. This is where the wonderful view of the **Burbage Valley** opens up, revealing large boulders, tors, and the impressive rocky edge high up on the horizon. Head past the next footbridge, keeping the river on your right and following the simple path at the side of the water. This takes you upstream towards **Burbage Bridge**.

④ Cross over the river using the footbridge and head up the path into the woods. Follow the path around to the right, joining a track that leads you to a road. Cross over here and pick up the route at the other side, entering the National Trust's **Longshaw Estate**. Walk beyond the visitor centre (there's the chance of refreshments and toilets here if you need them) and head through a

The walk through the National Trust's Longshaw Estate passes grazing animals and thriving woods.

gate before taking the path on the right leading down to a lake.

⑤ At the lake, turn off the main path and follow the sign to the left for **Yarncliff** and proceed through the gate. You'll now cross a grassed area dotted with ferns and pine trees, with **Granby Wood** on the right. Several younger oak trees are developing here, too. Head towards more trees and pick up the track leading to the left. When you head over a stream, take the path that branches off to the right. The main body of trees is kept on your right as you press on through a grassy area that often houses sheep and cows in the summer months. You'll walk past ferns and trees and eventually come to a wall with a gate – head through here into **Yarncliff Wood**.

⑥ You'll now be at the top of a steep slope that falls away to your right. There's a wall above you on your left and a view down to the valley below on the right. Stick to the path and continue straight ahead, following it when it bends down to the right and begins to descend some steps. After a brief bend to the left, there's another turn to the right leading to another series of steps that take you down the hill. A steep valley now descends to your left and you can hear a river flowing down it. The path brings you out at a road. Cross it carefully and head to the left for a short distance before picking up the path on your right and walking further down the hill. This path brings you back out at the café where the walk started.

What to look out for –

Burbage Brook

If you're walking here on a weekday during term time, it's possible you'll see a school group on the banks of Burbage Brook. This is a very popular place for teachers to bring geography students of all ages to complete a range of fieldwork activities connected with rivers. The key attraction here is the contrast between features of the river over a relatively short distance. Students can walk up to a steep, fast-flowing section of Burbage Brook where the high energy of floodwaters can transport large rocks down the slope. Along the section of the river where this walk passes, a gentler Burbage Brook is visible. The river does not have as much pace here and a key feature are the meanders which erode material on the faster-flowing

Burbage Brook.

outside of the bends and deposit rocks on the inside of the bends, where the water flows more slowly. A little further on, there's the opportunity to study waterfalls and the formation of a gorge, while upstream the damage to rocks caused by frost shattering can be seen in the huge boulders that have been broken off the gritstone "edge" framing the valley. While many children visiting here will be measuring the size of material in the river bed and the velocity of the water, others will simply want a paddle in the stream. This is a popular place to go for a summer picnic and a play in the water. Fortunately for everyone concerned, there's often an ice cream van parked up on the road, in easy walking distance of Burbage Brook.

Autumn is the best time to enjoy the far-reaching view from High Bradfield.

11 High Bradfield

3.7miles/6km

As the leaves turn golden, a walk through the woodlands surrounding Agden Reservoir reveals some cracking views of Peak District moors and farmland. Apart from the outstanding views out across the moors of the Peak District National Park's eastern fringe, there is plenty of local history to immerse yourself in if you want to explore further.

autumn

The Facts

Time 2 hours.

Terrain Some steep sections on well-established paths.

Starting point Jane Street, High Bradfield. (Grid reference SK 267926).

How to get there & parking High Bradfield is found to the north west of Sheffield, between the A616 and the A57. Jane Street is the road which has the pub and church on it. There is free street parking, though at times when the pub and church are busy you may have to travel a little further along the road for a space. (**Sat nav** S6 6LG).

Map Ordnance Survey OL1: The Peak District Dark Peak Area.

Refreshments The Old Horns pub is a great place to eat, with wonderful views from the beer garden. ☎ 01142 851207 www.theoldhorns.co.uk.

The Walk

❶ Make your way along cobbled **Jane Street**, passing the pub and heading for the church. Just before you reach the churchyard, take the path on the left, go through the gate and walk down the hill. Turn right and head along the terraced path before passing through another gate and proceeding down a short set of steps. There's a choice of paths; take the one on the right and head across the field. At the end of the fields, go through the gate and cross the road, picking up the path at the other side.

❷ After walking down the path, you'll come to a wooden bridge that takes you across the overflow from **Agden Reservoir**. Follow the path around to the left and stick to it as it goes past the park in **Low Bradfield** and brings you out at a road.

❸ Turn right onto the road and when you get to **Windy Bank** turn right again, following the sign for **Derwent Valley** and **Strines**. After walking beyond the dam wall, look out for the path on the right that takes you onto a path at the side of the reservoir.

❹ Head into the wooded area beside the reservoir. This is a simple path to follow, with the reservoir close by on the right. When you come to a fork in the path, take the one on the right. The path continues at the side of the reservoir, taking you alongside a moss-covered dry-stone wall amidst plenty of crunchy

autumn

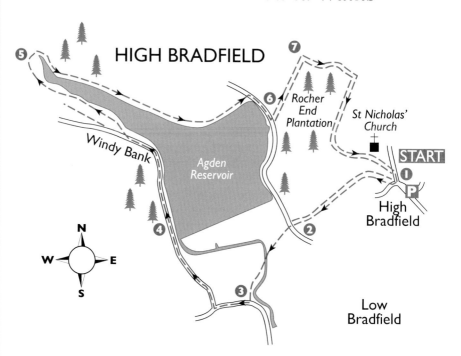

autumnal leaves. The path takes you up a small climb away from the reservoir briefly but then veers down to the head of the reservoir. Pass through a gate and turn left, heading towards the river you can hear flowing in the distance.

5 Take the footbridge crossing the river. Once you're at the other side of it, head up the bank and go through the gate, turning right onto the track at the other side. Continue along this path, with a dry-stone wall on the right that is eventually replaced by a metal fence. Soon after, there is a path on the right you should follow. It heads through a gate onto Yorkshire Water land by the reservoir once more. This permissive path takes you to the edge of the water and you need to turn left once you're there. This is a really pleasant waterside part of the walk, passing pine trees and enjoying lovely views across the reservoir. It will eventually bring you out at a road.

6 Turn right onto the road and look out for path number 93 on the left – it's just before you get to the bridge and from it you can see the dam wall and reservoir on the right. The path takes you up the hill through **Rocher End Plantation**. It's a steep climb, with trees turning autumnal colours all around.

7 Head through a kissing gate and take the path on the right that heads

Heading back towards the church at High Bradfield.

slightly downhill at first. It takes you over a stream as it bends away to the right. Pass through another gate and follow the path to the right once more before continuing ahead on an obvious route. There's a steep climb here, but as the path turns to the right it levels out. There are some beautiful views here out to the right over the reservoir to the moors beyond. The path you're walking on rises gently, while there is a steep drop down to your right. Go through a gap in the wall and you'll be in the churchyard at **High Bradfield**. Follow the footpath around the church and out of the gates at the far side to find yourself back on **Jane Street** where the walk started. On the way out of the church, look out for the unusual looking building on your left. This is the **Watch House**, built in 1745 to allow friends and relatives of the recently deceased to watch over the churchyard in case bodysnatchers should come to remove the dead. One of few such buildings to survive in the country, the **Watch House** is now a listed building.

autumn

What to look out for –

St Nicholas' Church

The peaceful churchyard at St Nicholas' Church is a tranquil place to walk through – you pass it at the end of this stroll. This beautiful countryside to the north of Sheffield was the scene of a terrible disaster back in March 1864 when nearby Dale Dyke Dam broke as the reservoir was being filled for the first time. The resulting torrent of water that surged down the valley washed away buildings in its path as it headed towards Sheffield and beyond. On that day, 240 people lost their lives and 600 buildings were damaged. Few people have heard about the Sheffield Flood. Indeed, one local school studying the disaster refers to it as the Forgotten Flood. At the time, it received very little press coverage outside the immediate area. Some people have claimed this is because it affected working class people in the north of the country. The memorials to the victims of the flood are little known and remarkably understated as well. Out at Dale Dyke Dam, there is a small plaque marking the site of the original wall close to where the current dam wall was rebuilt some years after the tragedy. And inside the church at High Bradfield there is

a memorial on the wall, which you can see if the church is open. The extensive churchyard contains the graves of families that were decimated by the catastrophic flood and as you walk along the path you'll see a small sign pointing you towards flood graves. This is also the final resting place of William Horsfield, the man who discovered the crack in the wall and raised the alarm. He survived the flood and died in the parish 17 years later.

Bilberry Reservoir has a charming view to match its name.

12 Holme
4 miles/6.4km

The walk around Holme rewards you with two types of view. There's the intimate picture of Bilberry Reservoir framed by the valley that encloses it, and there's the rolling expanse of moors leading down towards the towns and villages of West Yorkshire. This is a lovely walk around a series of reservoirs, passing beneath trees in full autumnal colour.

PEAK DISTRICT *Year Round Walks*

autumn

The Facts

Time 2 hours.

Terrain A mixture of waterside paths, grassy fields and small country roads.

Starting point The car park at Ramsden Reservoir. (Grid reference SK 115057).

How to get there & parking Head for Holmbridge on the A6024, turning up the small country road signed for Ramsden Reservoir. Park in the main car park. (**Sat nav** HD9 2QW).

Map Ordnance Survey OL1: The Peak District Dark Peak Area.

Refreshments When you arrive at Holme, a short diversion up the road brings you to the Fleece Inn on Woodhead Road. ☎ 01484 683449 www. fleeceinnholme.co.uk. **Postcode** HD9 2QG.

The Walk

❶ From the car park, head to the road and turn right onto it, heading for the dam wall. Cross over the dam, with **Brownhill Reservoir** on your right and **Ramsden Reservoir** on the left. Head across the dam wall to the far side, enjoying the view across the water of deciduous trees in full colour during autumn.

❷ Enter the wood at the far side of the dam wall, turning right onto a path and crossing the reservoir overflow. The path heads round to the right, with fences at either side. As the path rises into the wood, there is once again the opportunity to take in views of glorious trees. Soon the path bends to the left and it's important to ignore paths heading off to the left. Stick to the main path, following signs for the **Kirklees Way**. The path becomes rocky as it heads down a short slope towards a river. Cross over the wooden footbridge, looking out for the waterfall, and climbing up the other side of the valley. Follow the **Kirklees Way** as it takes you across a series of fields, revealing a view of moors and the **Holme Moss transmitter** behind you. The path becomes narrower and hemmed in as you approach Holme.

❸ At the village, turn left onto the road. The pub is a short way further up the road if you want to pay a visit, but if not you need to turn up the second road on the right, walking up **Meal Hill**. Walk up this lane, with houses on either

58

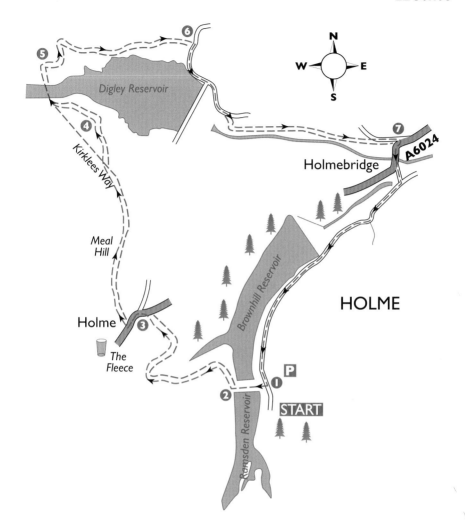

side of you. Look out, though, for the path on the right that leads away from the homes and over fields. Pass from field to field, sticking to the well-signed **Kirklees Way** as it takes you up the hill towards **Digley Reservoir**. Before long, you'll be able to see the reservoir laying at the end of the path ahead of you. Take the path on the right and head down to the edge of the reservoir.

4 The path crosses a stream and brings you to the edge of **Digley Reservoir**, where you should turn left onto a more established track. Head over another stream and through a gate before walking down a series of steps to the place where you'll cross **Digley Reservoir**. Approaching the reservoir, you pass

autumn

On the walk back to the car park, enjoy the view down to Brownhill Reservoir.

through a gate on the right and go by a series of picnic benches that would make a lovely place to stop. Continue to make your journey to the other side of **Digley Reservoir**.

5 The route across the dam wall of **Bilberry Reservoir** is very picturesque, with a fabulous view greeting you on your left. Once you've enjoyed the surprisingly pleasing secret view of **Bilberry Resevoir**, take the path up the hill at the other side, turning right onto the track. Continue ahead along this track, keeping **Digley Reservoir** on your right. Stick to this obvious path, pressing on up some steps and onwards, with fields on your left and the water down to your right. You'll pass an old quarry on the left.

6 The path brings you out at a road, where you need to turn right and head towards **Digley Reservoir's dam wall**. Keep to the main road and do not go across the wall, taking the path just after it on the right. The path heads down into a wood and over a wall, turning to the right and eventually joining with a larger track in the valley bottom. After you descend steps to join this track, turn left onto it and stick to it as you press ahead into **Holmbridge**. Passing houses and walking by a cricket pitch, you'll come to the main A6024 road opposite a church.

7 Turn right onto the road and look for the left turn soon after, signed to **Ramsden Reservoir**. Shortly after you will come to a T-junction and should turn right. Head up a gentle hill and you'll soon be walking by the side of **Brownhill Reservoir**. This is a gentle end to the walk in a scenic part of the Peak District, bringing you back to the car park at **Ramsden Reservoir**.

What to look out for –

Transmission masts

While you enjoy the longer views from elevated positions on the walk, it's hard not to notice the two huge transmitters that dominate the horizon. The nearest to you is the Holme Moss transmitter, with the one further away being Emley Moor.

The Holme Moss transmitter.

The Holme Moss transmitter is the highest in the country. The station itself is positioned some 524m above sea level, while the mast reaches 228m in height. This transmitting station is now exclusively for FM and DAB radio coverage and because of its height the area covered is huge. The transmissions cover all of Yorkshire and Lancashire, along with Greater Manchester and Cheshire. Signals from here can also be heard in London to the south and the Scottish borders to the north.

The 330m concrete tower you can see away in the distance is the Emley Moor mast, which is now a Grade II listed building. The tallest freestanding structure in the UK, it's actually the fourth tallest tower in Europe and the 24th tallest tower in the world. The first mast at Emley Moor was constructed in 1956 and was replaced by a taller version in 1964. But in 1969, the combination of strong winds and the weight of ice resulted in the collapse of that 385m tower. Work started on the current concrete tower in the same year and it began transmitting TV signals in 1971. The TV coverage of the Emley Moor mast is the largest of any in the UK, sending signals to most of Yorkshire over an area of 10,000km².

There are plenty of deciduous trees on this route, creating autumnal charm around Stanton in Peak.

13 Stanton in Peak

3.4 miles/5.5km

Through woodland and across scenic moors, this walk takes you to a mysterious Bronze Age stone circle known as Nine Ladies, traditionally believed to depict nine ladies turned to stone as a penalty for dancing on a Sunday. Enjoy the spectacular views this beautiful part of the southern Peak District offers.

Time 1 hour 30 minutes.

Terrain Some gentle climbs along well-established paths.

Starting point The lay-by at the highest point of Lees Road. (Grid reference SK 246641).

How to get there & parking Stanton in Peak is found just off the A6 between Matlock and Rowsley. There is lay-by parking on Lees Road, around 300m east of Stanton in Peak. (**Sat nav** DE4 2LS).

Map Ordnance Survey OL24: The Peak District White Peak Area.

Refreshments The Flying Childers is a popular pub, found at Stanton in Peak. ☎ 01629 636333. www.flyingchilders.com. **Postcode** DE4 2LW.

The Walk

1 Having parked up, continue walking along the road, away from Stanton in Peak and down the hill. Enjoy views of the moors, with **Rowsley** visible down in the valley. You'll soon see piles of rocks on the left, signifying the start of a working quarry and you may encounter some lorry-based activity as you make your way down. Just after the quarry entrance, take the footpath on the right; there are steps to take you over the wall. The path leads you into a small wood which at this time of year allows you to enjoy a 'crunchy leaves' walk surrounded by a blaze of colour. Head straight up the hill and pick up the narrower path at the top that leads through brambles.

Just before the halfway point of the walk, you'll come across a huge boulder.

2 Stick to this route, which has a fence on the right-hand side. There are far-reaching views to be had off to the left through the trees, a view that gets better as more leaves fall. You get brought to an old tower, with the path heading left of it. Known as the **Earl Grey Tower**, it was dedicated to the Reform Act of 1832 that restructured

autumn

the electoral system. As you come to **Stanton Moor Edge**, owned by the National Trust, the route passes through lots of browning bracken.

3 Just before you reach a large boulder, follow the path as it turns sharply to the right. You'll still have the fence to your right, and as you move away from the trees there are expansive views opening up on the left.

4 When you get brought out at a country road, turn right onto it. Look out for the path on the right leading onto the moor once again, and follow it up the bracken-strewn route. Pass the remains of an old quarry on the left and press on up a sandy path, with the fading colours of heather on either side. When you get to a crossroads of paths, press straight ahead. Continue along here, passing several silver birch trees along the way before you get to the **Nine Ladies** stone circle. There are interpretive boards giving you information about the stones and surrounding area along the route.

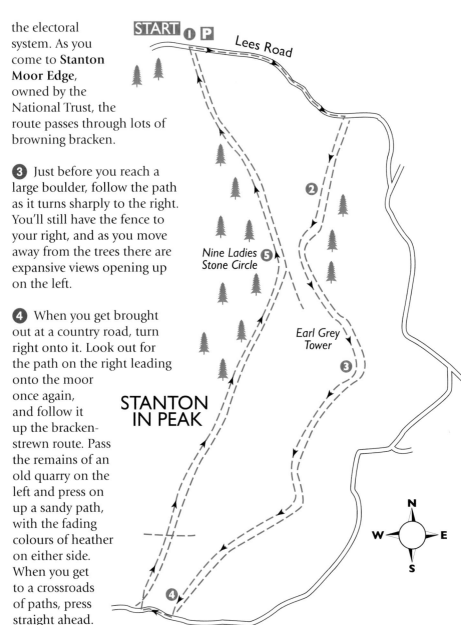

START ❶ 🅿
Lees Road

❷

Nine Ladies ❺
Stone Circle

Earl Grey
Tower
❸

STANTON
IN PEAK

❹

N
W — E
S

5 After having a good look around this important Bronze Age site, continue along the path leading away from the stone circle. Pass through a gate and continue straight ahead through the wood, keeping an eye out for resident squirrels getting ready for the winter. Follow the path as it heads across a couple of farming fields, and you'll be brought out at the lay-by where you started.

What to look out for –

Nine Ladies stone circle

As is the case with many other stone circles around the country, there is little evidence to establish precisely why the Nine Ladies were placed here on Stanton Moor and exactly how they were used. Many theories abound, including that it was a meeting place, a venue for ceremonies, somewhere burials took place or territory marker. The local legend tells of how nine ladies were all turned to stone after they were discovered dancing on a Sunday. But even if the far-fetched tale of petrifying females were possible, it does not account for the 1977 discovery of a tenth stone now lying flat on the ground. As you walk around Stanton Moor you will be able to get a feel for the wealth of Bronze Age remains that can be seen on the landscape. The Nine

Ladies stone circle is the most famous and easily recognised but there are over 70 stone cairns in this area, giving it a special importance to those involved in excavations and research about the Bronze Age. The single stone sitting around 40m from the Nine Ladies is called the King Stone and was mentioned by Charles Dickens in *The Pickwick Papers*. Look out for the graffiti carved into it many years ago by somebody called Bill Stumps. The local legend tells how the King Stone was once a fiddler playing music for the dancing ladies on the Sabbath. He too was turned to stone as a punishment for his lack of respect. Today, the Nine Ladies and the King Stone are looked after by English Heritage.

The Tissington Trail.

14 Tissington
6.1 miles/9.8km

Head out beneath autumnal skies by the side of colourful trees, and over farming fields to a charming village. The first section of the walk takes you along a former railway known as the Tissington Trail. It's a popular route with walkers, cyclists and those heading out on horses. From the very first few steps of the walk, you'll be able to see the first of many bridges that allowed pedestrians and traffic to cross over the railway. But keep a keen eye out for the less obvious but just as fascinating clues about the local area's railway and industrial heritage.

The Facts

Time 3 hours.

Terrain Fields and stiles to negotiate and a steep climb towards the end.

Starting point The car park at Tissington, next to the Tissington Trail. (Grid reference SK 17765205).

How to get there & parking Tissington is located just off the A515, between Newhaven and Ashbourne. From the centre of Tissington, the pay and display car park is well signposted and there are plenty of spaces there. (**Sat nav** DE6 1RA).

Map Ordnance Survey OL24: The Peak District White Peak Area.

Refreshments The walk passes through Parwich, where you will find the Sycamore Inn. ☎ 01335 390212. www.robinsonsbrewery.com/sycamoreparwich. **Postcode** DE6 1QL.

The Walk

❶ To begin the walk, make your way over to the **Tissington Trail**, and turn left onto it, walking in the direction of **Parsley Hay**. Almost immediately, you head under the first bridge and start to gain a feel for how this used to be a railway line that linked London with rural Derbyshire. On the left, look out for the deposits of volcanic ash once hidden by soil before being exposed by a conservation group. Keep your eyes and ears on the alert for cyclists; on this stretch of the walk it can be easy to get distracted as the far-reaching views of local farmland opens up to the left and right. The track continues and is easy to follow, over embankments and through cuttings that were blasted away when the line was being built. Pass beneath another bridge and the path bends round to the left. Soon after, another bridge signals a twist to the right. Make your way past a farm on the left, all the time sticking to the well-defined **Tissington Trail**. Further along the former train line you will see a large house up the embankment on the left. At this point you're shadowing close to the A515. Around 300 metres ahead there is a path on the right signed to **Parwich Lees** and it's here that you leave the **Tissington Trail**.

❷ The new path takes you down a slope into farming fields. Follow the route signed for **Parwich Lees** which takes you to the right across one field and through a gap in the wall. In the second field, keep to the left and climb to the corner of

autumn

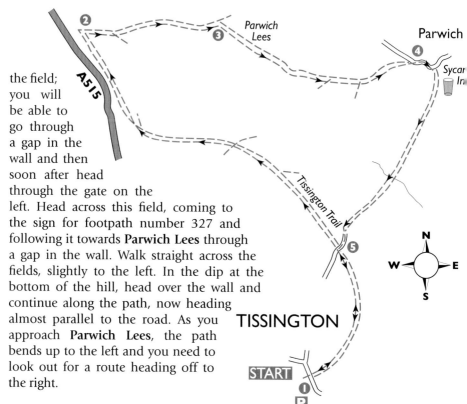

the field;
you will
be able to
go through
a gap in the
wall and then
soon after head
through the gate on the
left. Head across this field, coming to
the sign for footpath number 327 and
following it towards **Parwich Lees** through
a gap in the wall. Walk straight across the
fields, slightly to the left. In the dip at the
bottom of the hill, head over the wall and
continue along the path, now heading
almost parallel to the road. As you
approach **Parwich Lees**, the path
bends up to the left and you need to
look out for a route heading off to
the right.

❸ The change of direction takes you up
to the large house and you pass to the right of it. The path is simple to follow
over these rolling fields, and you'll find yourself climbing over a few stiles to
negotiate the walls. Eventually, the path will turn into a more substantial track
with fences on either side. At the bottom of this track look out for two paths;
you need to take the one heading right towards **Parwich**. Head down the hill
and across a small stream at the bottom before making your way towards the
road. This is **Parwich**, where there's a pub if you're in need of refreshment.

❹ Turn right onto the road and walk into the village. After a few metres, you'll
see a sign pointing off to the right towards **Tissington**. This leads you to a field
on the right-hand side of a house, with the path you need to follow heading
up the hill. At the top, pass through the gap in the wall and continue as it leads
you through fields at the other side. There are some very clear markers to look
out for as you are led through the fields, down into a dip and then up the other
side. Before you reach the top of the hill there's a marker indicating you should
head left, and beyond this you'll soon come to the **Tissington Trail** again.

autumn

The villages around Tissington are framed by limestone walls and rolling fields.

5 Head through the gate and turn left onto the **Tissington Trail**. Walking along the track, you'll eventually come to the first railway bridge you saw at the beginning of the walk and the car park close to the village of **Tissington**. If you have time to explore **Tissington**, you should have a look around. There is a very pleasant centre of the village, complete with a scenic pond and a tea room where you can enjoy a rest and something to eat.

What to look out for –

Railway heritage

The original railway line was built by the London and North Western Railway in 1899 to link the towns of Buxton and Ashbourne. The line was popular with passengers initially, enjoying an especially busy decade with ramblers in the 1930s. It also allowed an important 'milk train' to set off for London every day, taking produce from Peak District dairy farms to quench the thirst of the capital. But as the post-war period brought in the age of the car, the line began to suffer just as  dozens of others did up and down the country. Normal passenger services stopped in 1954, and although some specials continued to operate, the final train ran along here in 1963. The Tissington Trail opened in 1971 and is now part of a popular network of off-road cycle routes in the Peak District, which includes the High Peak Trail, Monsal Trail and Longdendale Trail.

Dry-stone walls near Litton.

15 Litton
3.9 miles/6.3km

Litton is a fabulous place from which to base an autumnal walk and there will be plenty of trees changing colour here towards the end of the year. Although close to the main road, Litton doesn't pull in the tourist crowds to the degree that nearby Tideswell does. This ensures that it remains a quieter visit, away from its neighbour's tourist gaze. It's well worth journeying to though and is fairly well equipped for a settlement of its size with a shop, post office and pub. Often overlooked in favour of the nearby Monsal Trail and popular Tideswell, you may find solitude on this stroll.

The Facts

Time 2 hours.

Terrain Some steep paths and uneven ground.

Starting point The centre of Litton on Church Lane. (Grid reference SK 162752).

How to get there & parking Litton is found just off the A623, close to Tideswell. There is roadside parking on Church Lane in the centre of the village. (**Sat nav** SK17 8RA).

Map Ordnance Survey OL24: The Peak District White Peak Area.

Refreshments The Red Lion at Litton is well worth checking out and is easily spotted from the main road when you walk past. ☎ 01298 871458. www.theredlionlitton.co.uk. **Postcode** SK17 8QU. If you are passing through Tideswell and want a good selection of specialist local cakes, a visit to Tindalls of Tideswell is a must (☎ 01298 871351 **Postcode** SK17 8NU).

The Walk

1 From **Christ Church** on **Church Lane**, head down the hill and you'll come to a junction which marks the centre of the village. Turn left here and continue on ahead, passing a phone box and the **Methodist church**. Shortly after this, on the right there are some steps leading over a wall next to a house. This marks a rather discreet start for footpath 347, signed for **Cressbrook Dale**.

2 Once you leave the road, you start your trek over the first of several fields. Almost immediately, you get a feel for being in the heart of limestone country. You can gaze to the left and see some impressive outcrops over at Peter's Stone. Go over a wall at the end of this first field and turn left onto a track before taking the path on the right soon after. You'll find yourself in another field and should follow the path alongside the wall. When the wall comes to an end, the path veers off to the left. You now head down the hill towards the charming **Tansley Dale**, which you'll soon be in once you've climbed the stile in another wall.

3 As you descend down **Tansley Dale**, you can't help but be impressed by the enclosed nature of this small dale, with plenty of limestone being exposed and the odd tree living a solitary life. It's worth looking around at the limestone

autumn

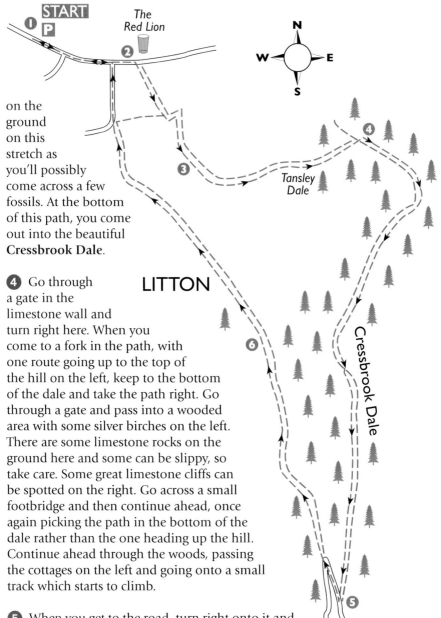

on the ground on this stretch as you'll possibly come across a few fossils. At the bottom of this path, you come out into the beautiful **Cressbrook Dale**.

4 Go through a gate in the limestone wall and turn right here. When you come to a fork in the path, with one route going up to the top of the hill on the left, keep to the bottom of the dale and take the path right. Go through a gate and pass into a wooded area with some silver birches on the left. There are some limestone rocks on the ground here and some can be slippy, so take care. Some great limestone cliffs can be spotted on the right. Go across a small footbridge and then continue ahead, once again picking the path in the bottom of the dale rather than the one heading up the hill. Continue ahead through the woods, passing the cottages on the left and going onto a small track which starts to climb.

5 When you get to the road, turn right onto it and continue on up. At the bend in the road that doubles back to the left, you need to take the path that goes straight on, once again taking you into the woods. After around 200 metres there is a fork in the path and you take the route

Moss-strewn walls and fallen leaves add to the atmosphere of this wonderful autumn stroll.

climbing the hill on the left. This is a steep section which involves you climbing a series of steps. When you reach the top, you'll be brought out at a thin path that takes you by the edge of the woods.

6 You should follow the path as it leaves the woods and takes you across a couple of fields. Go over some steps and cross a large field, then at the end of it you go straight across a track into another field. You're now going down into a small dip across two fields, but for the push up the other side towards Litton you go through a wall and head directly up. At the top, go over the steps in the wall and turn left onto a track, which will bring you out at a road pretty much straight away. Turn right onto this and follow it back into **Litton**. Turn left at the main road, pass the phone box and look out for the **Church Lane**, which is where you set out from.

What to look out for –

autumn

Christ Church, Litton

Christ Church is a relatively recent building as far as places of worship go, dating back to the 1920s. It was built using money donated by a Miss Penfold of Sterndale House, using Stancliffe Stone. Unlike many churches, the building in Litton is surrounded by really well kept gardens and in them you'll be able to see a stone cross. Another notable sight is the 18th-century font inside the church, which is older than the building itself. Unsurprisingly given the wonderful building and its fabulous surroundings, this is a very popular venue for weddings and has also been used to host concerts and other events. Litton gives thanks on an annual basis through its well-dressing, which sees a decorative board creatively designed with petals and seeds with a theme each year. But despite there being some days that pull in the crowds, there's generally enough room for parking on Church Lane. Even if it is busy there, you won't have to go far before you find a space. It's one of the best things about Litton – there's plenty to do and it's a charming place without the throngs that cluster around some of the other Peak District villages.

The control tower at Carsington Water.

16 Carsington

8 miles/12.9km

This is a long circular walk that may challenge younger members of the family. But even in the coldest of weather, it makes for a cracking day out as you enjoy the local wildlife, take in scenic views, spend time in the playground and savour an ice cream back at the visitor centre! As you walk around the water's edge, enjoy the woodland and admire the abundance of wildlife, it's easy to forget that Carsington Water is a man-made landscape. This is a lovely walk for the whole family to take part in and is largely on the level, using easy-to-follow footpaths.

Time 3 hours 30 minutes.

Terrain The tracks are easy to follow and the terrain is good, but there are some short, steep sections and tricky bends on the descent.

Starting point The visitor centre at Carsington Water. There is a pay and display car park. (Grid reference SK 241515).

How to get there & parking Carsington Water is the large body of water at the southern end of the Peak District, between the A515 and the A6. It is located just off the B5035 at Knockerdown. Park in the main car park near the visitor centre. (**Sat nav** DE6 1ST).

Map Ordnance Survey OL24: The Peak District White Peak Area.

Refreshments A range of places to eat are available at the Carsington Visitor Centre, including the Mainsail Restaurant, Watermark Café and Splatz. Contact the centre for more information. ☎ 01629 540363. www.visitcarsington.co.uk .

The Walk

1 Setting out from the visitor centre, the route is well-established and there are plenty of signs to keep you on track along the circular route. The main thing to remember is that you're going around in a clockwise direction, which means the water should be on your right. Follow the sign for the **Wildlife Centre** and **Sheepwash** as you move away from the visitor centre. The path will take you past the cycle hire centre on your right and you'll soon become used to spotting the blue signs that help you throughout the route. Keep following them towards the **Wildlife Centre**.

2 Turn off to the right soon and walk towards the **Bombing Tower**. Follow the track as it climbs a small hill and then goes down into a dip. This up-down pattern is repeated a few times, all with a conservation area on your right. Some of the climbs are fairly steep. For a while you will be walking along the national cycle route number 547, though you should leave these when the blue signs tell you to and stick to the round **Carsington cycle trail**.

3 You'll soon come to another car park. Follow the track beyond this and you'll find yourself on a section mirroring the course of the road. When you leave the roadside, you'll drop down into a wooded area and return to the

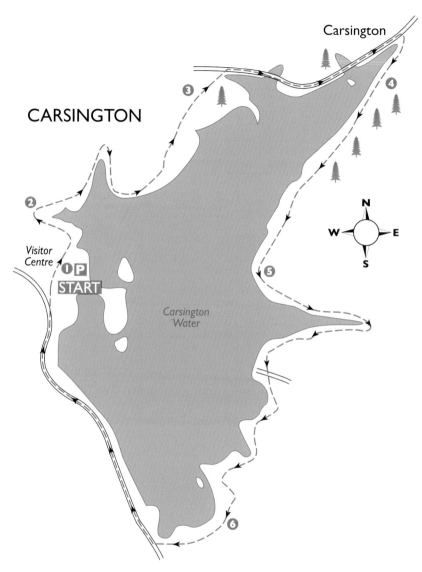

reservoir. All along this route there are plenty of places to sit and rest if it's not too chilly.

4 Further along the track, you'll come to a gate which takes you into a grassier landscape and soon returns you to the tree-lined reservoir path through another gate. There are a few ups and downs before you're taken through two more gates, followed by a steep descent.

The track takes you on a circumnavigation of Carsington Water, though you do sometimes leave the water's edge.

5 Continue to follow the blue signs on the route, and you'll get brought out at a track where you need to turn left and climb up the hill. As you make your way up, look out for the turning on the right that you'll soon need to take. There's a steep uphill section now, but you'll be rewarded by the view of the dam wall and the visitor centre opposite. It's a lovely sight to gaze upon, and you can now see your route for the remaining part of the walk.

6 There's a steep descent on this section, and it bends around at the bottom to bring you out at another car park. From here, you follow the track onto the dam wall and walk straight across this large, impressive structure that retains the vast amounts of water on your right. At the end of the wall, the track bends around to the right and you head past the sailing club. There's a road here you need to carefully cross, but once at the other side you'll soon find yourself back at the visitor centre. Before you get there, the younger members of your group might like to spend time in the playground you pass on the way!

What to look out for –

Man-made beauty

The path heading along the dam wall.

There's nothing natural about having this stretch of water here, even though it fits in so spectacularly. This is the England's ninth biggest reservoir, serving cities of the Midlands, and its history is a relatively recent one compared to others in the Peak District. Plans were first drawn up for a reservoir here at Carsington in the 1960s, though it was 1979 – the year Margaret Thatcher came to power – that work actually started at this site. Initially, the construction didn't go as planned. In 1984 there was a partial collapse of the dam wall. Thankfully, it was before any water had been taken into the reservoir. It was so serious a failure that the whole dam wall was taken away and another one was built. Work on the new dam wall wasn't started until 1989 – ten years after initial work on the reservoir started. The grand opening by Queen Elizabeth II took place 1992 – two years after Margaret Thatcher resigned. Today, as well as being a water source, Carsington is a major centre for recreation. As well as being an obvious destination for cyclists, you're also likely to come across walkers, birdwatchers, fishermen, sailors, canoeists and windsurfers. Oh, and they've also held music concerts here as well! One more thing for you to look out for on your visit is the exhibition about water usage in the visitor centre. You'll never think about your toilets and sinks the same after you've had a look around! Make your winter walk at Christmas and you can time it to see carollers singing in the courtyard.

Walls in this part of the Peak District are made from gritstone.

17 Derwent Valley

4.5 miles/7.2km

As you're wandering beside the reservoirs of the Derwent Valley, it's easy to forget this is a man-made environment. This walk takes in the many different Peak District landscapes including farmland and woods, the open moorland of Pike Low and some great views of Ladybower Reservoir, Derwent Dam and the Dark Peak area. Visit in the winter months in the middle of the week and you might even have this lovely scenery to yourself. Wrap up warm and remember to take your camera!

Time 2 hours 15 minutes.

Terrain The tracks alongside the reservoirs are well established and easy-going, but expect things to get more challenging and possibly a little wet as you climb up onto the moors.

Starting point The car park at Fairholmes. (Grid reference SK 172893).

How to get there & parking The Derwent Valley is easy to find and signposted off the A57 at the eastern end of the Snake Pass. Continue to the end of the road to reach the Fairholmes car park. (**Sat nav** S33 0AQ).

Map Ordnance Survey OL1: The Peak District Dark Peak Area.

Refreshments When you finish your walk, you'll be glad of the little kiosk in the car park that's open all weathers and serves hot food, snacks and drinks.

The Walk

❶ Starting from **Fairholmes**, head beyond the visitor centre and shop, following signs for **The Dams**, and then turn right onto the road. Head along the quiet road, passing the impressive **Derwent Dam** on the left, and the road bends round to the right, allowing you to see **Ladybower Reservoir** down to your right. Pass **Old House Farm** on your left and continue pressing ahead on this pleasant route.

❷ Take the path on the left, where you enter **Wellhead**, part of the National Trust's High Peak Estate. This path rises up the hill and bends to the left, becoming a more established, though at times rocky, track. The valley down to the right and the tors up on the hill give this section of the walk a great feeling. Go through a gate as the path has embankments and trees on either side, then proceed through the next gate and follow the footpath sign to the left. Take a look out here for the gorse bushes, which flower yellow in winter, and carry on up the path and over a stile.

❸ When you reach the house at **Lanehead** on the left, follow the path straight ahead signed for **Derwent Moors**. You'll reach a grassy field at the top and the path you need here is the one forking to the right. Go through a gate at the other side and enter **Pike Low**, the start of the open moor. There are some great

winter

views from up here, including **Ladybower Reservoir** behind you. Stick to the path and follow the footpath sign as it bends to the right through an area rich with heather. The path continues to take you over the moors, following a ruined wall for a time and then bringing you to a more open section of the moor and taking you beyond a small plantation of pine trees. At the junction of footpaths, follow the sign for **Howden Dam**, press on over a stile and take in the view of **Derwent Dam** down on the left.

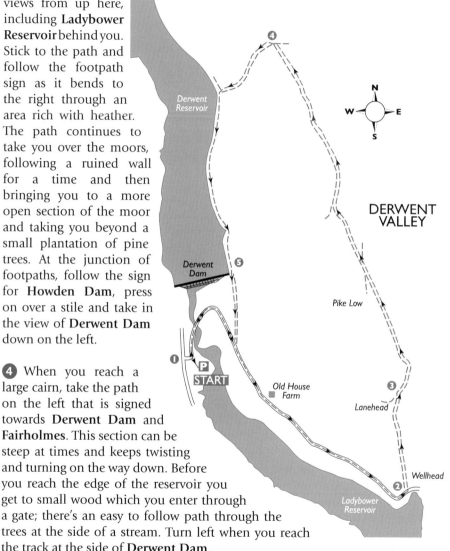

④ When you reach a large cairn, take the path on the left that is signed towards **Derwent Dam** and **Fairholmes**. This section can be steep at times and keeps twisting and turning on the way down. Before you reach the edge of the reservoir you get to small wood which you enter through a gate; there's an easy to follow path through the trees at the side of a stream. Turn left when you reach the track at the side of **Derwent Dam**.

⑤ At the dam wall, famous for the twin towers, take the path on the right and go down the steps that bring you to the foot of the dam wall. From here, cross the grass to the road and turn right onto it. Over the bridge, take the path on the left that will bring you back to the car park.

Gazing down to Derwent Reservoir.

What to look out for –

Derwent Dam

The building of this historic and iconic wall started in 1902. It was 14 years later when the water started to fill up the reservoir and eventually start to overflow, creating the picturesque sight that many people now enjoy a few weeks of every year. The wall was, of course, used as a dry run for the famous Dambuster raid in World War II, as preparation was made for blowing up German reservoirs with bouncing bombs. Some nine years after the war ended, there were planes flying over the dam wall at Derwent once more as cameras rolled for the filming of *The Dam Busters* movie. Making the flight scenes took two weeks and was extremely difficult because the Lancaster had to fly very low over the water and wall. To make filming more problematic, the Dambusters raid was at night and this made the manoeuvres even more dangerous. However, the Derwent action in the film was filmed during the day to make it safer –when you watch the film it appears to be at night because the film was overexposed. Seeing a Lancaster Bomber fly over the wall these days is a rare event, but it has happened a few times over the years. Several ceremonial flypasts have taken place to mark different events, and it certainly is a sight to behold, with the purring engine of the Lancaster providing a sound that can't be forgotten.

Dominating the horizon of the Hope Valley, the collapsed side of Mam Tor has been ravaged by landslips.

18 Castleton
4.2 miles/6.8km

Visit Castleton at Christmas and you're in for a real treat: the sight of decorated trees outside every shop combined with the smell of wood fires roaring in local homes gives a very festive feel. Time this right and you might even be able to combine your visit with one of the carol services in the local caverns that have become a regular festive treat for many. This walk takes you from the village to nearby Hope and back, all the while sticking to low-level paths in case the hills are knee-deep in snow. Castleton has something to offer all year round, but there's something special about being there on a clear, crisp day in winter.

winter

Time 2 hours 15 minutes.

Terrain The paths are easy to follow and low lying. There are a couple of roads to negotiate and after heavy rain, some of the paths may become muddy.

Starting point The main car park in the centre of Castleton. (Grid reference SK150829).

How to get there & parking The A6187 passes through Castleton, which is found to the west of Bamford, beyond Hope. Park in the village's main car park, close to the visitor centre. (Sat nav S33 8WH).

Map Ordnance Survey OL1: The Peak District Dark Peak Area.

Refreshments There are several coffee shops and tea rooms to enjoy in Castleton, but among the best is Three Roofs Café, opposite the visitor centre and main car park. ☎ 01433 620533. **Postcode** S33 8WN.

The Walk

1 From the car park, head for the main road and head in the direction of Hope, away from the dramatic hills of **Winnats Pass**.

2 Just before you leave **Castleton**, take the path on the right that is signed

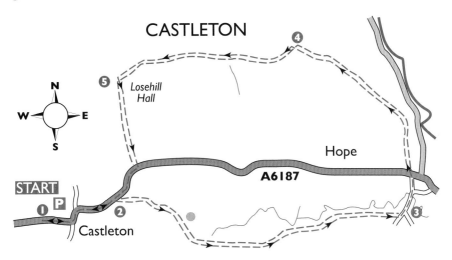

winter

Peveril Castle, cared for by English Heritage.

towards **Hope** and takes you down a track with limestone walls on each side called **The Lane**. With the cement works in the distance, you pass a farm where snowdrops grow in winter. Follow the track, with a small river on the left. Go through a gate and follow the path beyond a small wood before the path ventures away from the river into fields linked by stiles and gates; follow the path along this series of fields until you carefully cross the railway line, then pick up the route through the fields once more.

3 The path will bring you out at a road, where you turn left. Look out for the pinfold on your left at this point. Proceed along the road, over a bridge, and you'll come to the main road through **Hope**. Cross over the road and turn left, but take the footpath signed for **Losehill** you'll soon find on your right that leads between two buildings. This takes you past some houses, turn right at a road and pass **Hope Clinic** before picking up the path at the other side of the road. Continue following the path for **Losehill**, which is well signed and takes you across a bridge over the train track. Go through a couple of gates at the other side, press on past the farm and enjoy the views of this huge valley.

4 At the junction of paths, turn left. Follow the signs for **Castleton** and stick to this path that soon takes you down some steps and across a stream. Continue across the field on the other side and take the concession footpath in the field to the right as you approach **Spring House Farm**. Join a track for a short distance and then take the path off to the right that is signed for **Castleton**. As you head over a stream, you'll see fabulous views of **Mam Tor** ahead. Branch left when the track comes to a t-junction and you'll approach **Losehill Hall**.

5 Follow the track around to the left when you reach **Losehill Hall** and continue on this route, which will bring you out at the main road in **Castleton**. Turn right onto it and press on into the centre of **Castleton**, where the walk set out from. After you've finished this circular walk and wind up back in the village, you may like to kick back in one of the charming country pubs and take a look in local shops for specialist Blue John jewellery.

What to look out for –

The pinfold

An animal compound was a feature found in most medieval villages and you'll find a great example of one just as you're about to enter Hope. Look for the circular stone structure on your left. It has the appearance of a sheep pen, and that's pretty much what it was. Any animals that were found wandering off were rounded up and placed under lock and key in here until their owners came to claim them. To get the animal back, the owner would have to pay a fee that depended on how long the creature had been impounded. Feeding and watering costs were taken into account, along with the fee taken by the person looking after the pinfold. However, if the animal taken into the pinfold was left there for too long and not claimed, it could be sold at market in order to retrieve costs. The pinfold surviving at Hope gives a great insight into life gone by in this rural village.

Broomhead Reservoir.

19 Bolsterstone

4.2 miles/6.8km

Nestling on the very edge of the Peak District boundary, Bolsterstone is a quiet and charming village with Anglo Saxon roots and a long history. The village stocks can still be seen against the church wall. This walk takes you into the Peak District and around a reservoir surrounded by pine woodland – a perfect route for those crunchy winter mornings.

Time 2 hours.

Terrain Well marked paths that are easy to follow; a fairly steep descent down to the reservoir and then back up again at the end.

Starting point St Mary's Church, Bolsterstone. (Grid reference SK 270968).

How to get there & parking From Stocksbridge on the A616, follow local signs for Bolsterstone. There are free parking bays outside the church. (**Sat nav** S36 3ZN).

Map Ordnance Survey OL1: The Peak District Dark Peak Area.

Refreshments The Castle Inn is located at the start/finish point of the walk. ☎ 0114 2886300. **Postcode** S36 3ZB.

The Walk

1 As you look at the church, turn to the left and head away from the centre of the village along the road. Very soon you'll see **Heads Lane** turning off on the right and this is the route you need to follow. Walk beyond the **old school house** on the left and then keep on going on the lane, passing the impressive **Old Vicarage** as well. The **churchyard** you pass on the right is fairly large, once you walk by it you're into open countryside with farming fields, woods and moors opening up all around.

2 Continue heading out into the countryside but keep your eyes peeled for a path on the left where you head through a gate and down to a **farm**. When you get to the **farmhouse**, turn right following the yellow signs and walk to the side of the house, where you then turn left and go down across the farmyard to the gate. Going through this takes you into a field and you now need to follow the track downhill, with the reservoir coming into view ahead of you. Pass through another gate and as you reach the bottom of the field you need to aim for the trees in the bottom right of the field, climbing over a stile and into the wood. Follow the steep path down through the wood on a well-marked track and when you reach a junction of paths marked by a wooden post and two yellow signs – you need to take the one on the left.

3 Cross over a little stream and continue heading down to the woods until you are brought out at the road. Cross over and move a little to the left to pick

winter

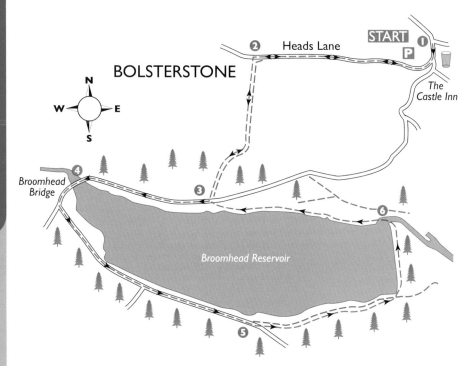

up the path at the other side. You're now on what is essentially the perimeter path of the reservoir. Turn right to begin your circumnavigation of **Broomhead**. There are some huge pine trees on this section of the walk, giving it a lovely feel, and you keep the water on your left as you continue your journey, eventually coming out at the road close to **Broomhead Bridge**.

❹ Turn left onto the road and go over the bridge. Soon after it you'll see a path on the left which once again takes you into the woods and on the path near the reservoir. Follow the path through the woodland, crossing over a wooden raised path close to the road and continuing straight ahead with the reservoir on your left. It's a straightforward route and it will eventually bring you to **New Road**.

❺ From here, head down the bridleway taking you into **Fox Hill Wood,** locally known as **Horse Wood**. You can now see the dam wall ahead of you on the left and when you reach it there is a gate on your left you need to go through so that you can join the path along the top of the dam wall. Make your way to the other side of the dam wall and head through a gate before crossing the bridge over the overflow for the reservoir.

6 You'll then see a track ahead of you and you need to turn left along it, following it as it gently goes up uphill. Turn left onto **Yewtrees Lane** and continue along here under the trees until you see the path on the right that you initially came down. Follow it up the hill through the wood and then over the stile and out onto the field. The track up the hill eventually brings you to the farm once more and the path turns right around the back of it before taking a left turn up onto **Heads Lane**. Turn right onto here and you'll find yourself walking back to the centre of **Bolsterstone**, where the walk started.

Pine woodland in South Yorkshire is explored as the walk goes near the reservoir.

What to look out for –

St Mary's Church

The church of St Mary dominates the village of Bolsterstone, just as it has since being built in 1879. A religious site, this dates back much further than that, though – people have worshipped here since the 12th century. Back in the 17th century, a small chapel stood here but it proved unpopular with locals who wanted a larger place. Building started in 1872, lasted seven years and cost £7,200. Modernisation took place in the years after it was first opened, new bells and an organ being installed in the 1880s while the lychgate was put up to mark the diamond jubilee of Queen Victoria back in 1897. From the road, on the right of the lychgate, look out for the Celtic cross that is the local war memorial, remembering the people who gave their lives in conflict. In the churchyard, see if you can spot the two rectangular stones that gave the village its name. Nobody is really sure where they came from, but these are known as the Bolster Stones.

Fernilee Reservoir.

20 *Fernilee Reservoir*

3.2 miles/5.1km

Despite being so close to Buxton, the wonders of the Goyt Valley are fairly well hidden unless you know where to look. You obviously can't miss spotting Fernilee Reservoir as you walk around it, but the historical significance and interest linked to this part of the Peak District is often associated with the things you can't see. This is an ideal place for a winter stroll – pick a day with clear skies and you're in for a real treat as the low sun reflects on the water. This wonderful landscape features woods, farms and reservoirs but can be a quiet place, ideal for enjoying a tranquil walk. It is popular with dog walkers – especially in the latter stages so you'll probably see a few dogs bounding about. With the water and woods, it's a canine paradise.

The Facts

Time 1 hour 30 minutes.

Terrain Well marked paths, rocky in places. Some gentle climbs and a steep one to finish. Can be muddy after a rainy period.

Starting point Fernilee Reservoir car park. (Grid reference SK 013756).

How to get there & parking North of Buxton, the A5004 has a road signed off to the west for the Goyt Valley. From the main road, head past Errwood Sailing Club, cross the dam wall and you'll find the main car park for Fernilee Reservoir at the other side. (**Sat nav** SK23 7HD).

Map Ordnance Survey OL24: The Peak District White Peak Area.

Refreshments None on the route. The Shady Oak at Fernilee is a popular place many walkers head to. ☎ 01663 733658. www.facebook.com/theshadyoakcountryinn. **Postcode** SK23 7HD.

The Walk

1 From the car park, head for the road and you'll see the footpath you need heading across the grass to **Fernilee Reservoir**. Go through a gate, again following the signs for the reservoir. The impressive sight of this long reservoir greets you and then you go through a kissing gate, following the path that leads you down to the water's edge. When you reach the track next to the reservoir, turn left onto it and continue along the route with the water on your right. Keep following the signs for **Fernilee** along the **Waterside Walk**. As you follow this route you'll pass a few streams entering the reservoir and there's a wood on the left with pine trees, squeaking and creaking. After a rocky section, head over a wooden footbridge and then the path leaves the reservoir and you climb up some steep steps.

2 When you reach a larger path at the top of the steps, turn right and follow the sign for **Fernilee** once again. This path will bring you back down the hill, getting you back towards the water.

3 When you get to a gate, go through it and turn right onto the road at the other side. When you get to the dam wall, turn right and head along it, taking time to enjoy the views across the water.

4 At the far side of the **Fernilee Reservoir** dam wall, look out for the overflow.

The route around Fernilee is a popular one for dog owners.

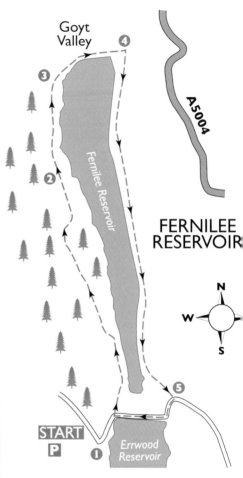

Goyt
Valley

Fernilee Reservoir

A5004

FERNILEE
RESERVOIR

N
W   S

START
P   ①

Errwood
Reservoir

Beyond the end of the dam wall, take the path on the right and you'll once again find yourself walking by the side the reservoir. You'll pass through a gate and there are a few benches that you pass on this stretch, making it an ideal place to stop for a snack. Continue until you get towards the end of the reservoir, when the imposing sight of **Errwood Reservoir** dam wall comes into view. Follow the track as it climbs

winter

steeply up the left side of the wall and comes out at a road.

⑤ When you reach the road, turn right onto it and follow it as you go by the sailing club and along the dam wall for **Errwood Reservoir**. At far side of the dam wall, follow the road up the hill to the junction and the car park is directly opposite.

What to look out for –

Fernilee Reservoir

Hidden below the twin reservoirs of Fernilee and Errwood, both of which you see on this walk, is a secret world that disappeared forever when the Stockport Water Corporation moved in during the 1930s. The first reservoir to be built was Fernilee, completed in 1938 to quench the thirst of Stockport and holding 4,940 million litres of water when full. The project cost £480,000 and was followed 30 years later by Errwood Reservoir, a £1.5 million construction holding 4,215 million litres of water. A compulsory purchase order saw the Stockport Corporation get hold of

the Errwood Estate in 1930 and the folk who lived in the now flooded houses started to move away slowly. An article in the *Nottingham Evening Post* from 1936 refers to the "final exodus" as the last six families moved out, most taking their possessions and livestock the short distance to Whaley Bridge and Kettleshulme. Looking at the reservoirs today, it's hard to imagine life carrying on many metres below the surface of what are now two very important stretches of water.

OTHER TITLES FROM COUNTRYSIDE BOOKS

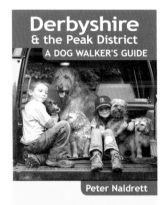

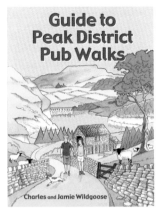

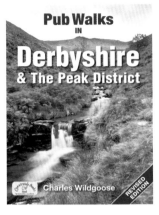

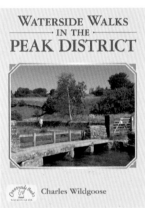

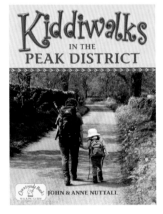

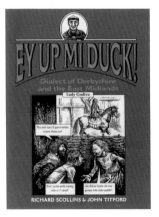

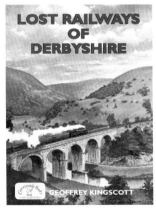

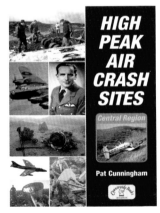

To see the full range of books by Countryside Books then visit
www.countrysidebooks.co.uk

Follow us on ![f] @ CountrysideBooks